Ski Tech's Guide to
Maintenance and Repair

Edited by Bill Tanler

John Muir Publications
Santa Fe, New Mexico

John Muir Publications, P.O. Box 613, Santa Fe, NM 87504

First edition. First printing

Library of Congress Cataloging-in-Publication Data
Ski tech's guide to maintenance and repair/edited by Bill Tanler.—
  1st ed.
        p.   cm.
    ISBN 0-945465-46-7
    1. Skis and skiing—Equipment and supplies—Maintenance and
repair.   I. Tanler, Bill. II. Ski tech.
GV854.E6S59   1989
686.7′693—dc20   89-42943
                                                   CIP

Distributed to the book trade by:

W. W. Norton & Company, Inc.
New York, New York

Cover photo: Diane Huntress
Cover design: Susan Surprise
Illustrations: Jim Finnell

Contents

Acknowledgments

Much of the material in *Ski Tech's Guide to Maintenance and Repair* was written originally for *Ski Tech* magazine and was adapted for this book by *Ski Tech* editors Carol Wright, Marc Sani, and Bill Tanler.

During the three years that this material was produced, numerous individuals in the ski industry provided information for many of the staff-written articles. While there are really too many to mention by name, several contributors do deserve special mention as the authors of most of the technical articles.

The ski tuning and repair material was written by Jim Deines, of Precision Ski, Inc., Frisco, Colorado, and Dana and Dan Brienza of Looney Tunes, Taos, New Mexico. Ed Chase and Blake Lewis of K2 also offered tuning suggestions.

Bob Gleason, of The Boot Doctor in Taos, New Mexico, wrote most of the alpine boot material, with Sven Coomer and service representatives of most of the boot companies contributing information.

Paul Parker, Bob Woodward, Rob Kiesel, and John Dostal wrote most of the Nordic material.

Carl Ettlinger of Vermont Ski Safety, Steve Hanft of Snow Summit, California, and Jackson Hogen provided most of the necessary details on ski bindings and boot and binding testing and the ASTM program.

Other contributors include Luanne Pfeiffer, who researched the material on ski poles, and Daniel Gibson, who helped edit, write, and assemble material for several chapters in this book. To all, especially those members of the ski industry not specifically mentioned here, your cooperation and patience made this book possible.

Introduction

Skis, boots, and bindings have undergone major improvements in recent years—design and cosmetic as well as technical—which have been made possible by the development of new, stronger synthetic materials. These technical improvements have resulted in fewer quality and performance differences between brands and between high-end and low-end models. All of the world's major ski manufacturers are capable of producing serviceable, quality products. Today, no skier should have trouble finding suitable skis at an affordable price. All alpine binding manufacturers are marketing models that are far superior to the best bindings available just five or ten years ago. And boot selection is largely a matter of fit and personal preference.

While better equipment is now available, it has become increasingly sophisticated. For example, sintered polyethylene base materials are more difficult to take care of than softer extruded base materials. We have learned that extra time invested in binding mounting and boot and binding system testing has resulted in a dramatic reduction in the number of lower leg injuries. It has made skiing safer. But this has placed greater responsibility on the performance of shop personnel.

Built-in boot fitting devices, as well as wider use of orthotics and boot fitting aids, have made it possible to offer every skier a comfortable fit without sacrificing performance. But the introduction of new designs and new materials in ski equipment has made it more difficult to service and repair the sophisticated products manufactured today.

As there is less difference in products brand to brand, service and maintenance have become even more important. For example, a well-tuned less expensive ski will outperform a neglected, more expensive ski. What happens in the back shop is all-important in helping skiers obtain the best possible performance from the equipment they buy.

This book is intended to help ski shop technicians do better, more knowledgeable work. It was also written for skiers who enjoy working on their own equipment. All of the tools available to the shop technician are available to the home mechanic.

As is true in all crafts, written instructions serve best as an introduction. All successful ski tuners and boot fitters have learned their trade by experimenting and practice. There is not necessarily one right way or one wrong way to tune a pair of skis. Two expert technicians may produce the same results with two different approaches to the same task. The most important first step is becoming familiar with the tools of the trade. With experience, you can become an expert.

PART I   ALPINE SKIS

1 *Hand Tuning*

The wider use of stone grinders and other sophisticated shop equipment has greatly reduced the time and labor involved in ski tuning. Yet no single machine has been developed which can replace an expert technician working with basic hand tools to turn out customized work and finely tuned skis.

As many ski retailers have discovered when working on neglected or "trashed" skis, modern shop equipment can handle heavy work quickly, producing a flat ski ready for hand finishing. Smaller shops, lacking the volume to justify a substantial investment in shop equipment, or individual skiers who simply want to coax the best possible performance out of their skis, have no choice but to do most of their work by hand.

The basic steps described here are for individual skiers who want to hand tune or make relatively minor repairs, for small shops with little or no repair or refinishing equipment, or for specialty shops that want to offer hand tuning as a service option. Subtle skills required to produce high-quality work are only acquired with experi-ence, practice, and some experimen-tation. New sintered bases and the acceptance of beveling as a positive contribution to ski performance have made ski repair and tuning a bit more complex. Still, basic hand-tuning techniques are relatively easy to learn.

Tools and Supplies

It is impossible to do good work without proper tools and supplies. Basic hand tuning equipment is not expensive. The individual items can be purchased from a variety of sources —ski equipment suppliers, hardware stores, building supply outlets, and the local supermarket.

At the most elementary level, for a simple touch-up, you may be able to get by with one or two good files, some fine grit silicon carbide paper, and a plastic scraper. But sooner or later, you will need every tool in your kit. And you will be pleased to have all your tuning supplies in one spot.

Every one of the following items will come in handy: a small propane

5

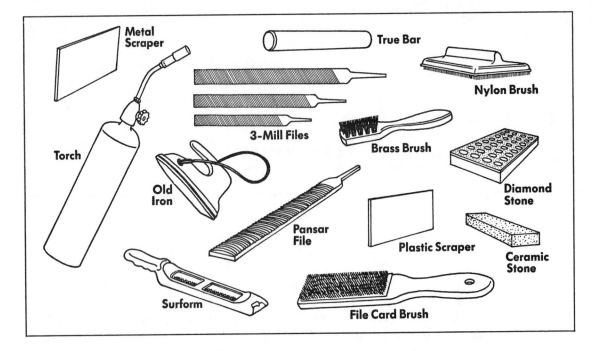

torch, a true bar, 12-inch, 8-inch, and 6-inch mill bastard files, one 10-inch body file/Pansar blade, one plastic scraper, one metal scraper, one Surform tool, a 4-inch ceramic or aluminum oxide stone, a 4-inch diamond stone, a file card, silicon carbide paper (80 to 320 grit), a riller bar, one brass brush, fiberlene paper or a lint-free rag, one nylon brush, an old iron, Scotch-brite or Fibertex pads, paper towels, and high-density polyethylene base repair materials.

Getting Set Up

If you are not working in a shop, find a well-ventilated and well-lit work spot with a sturdy bench. Good ventilation is important as you will be working with cleaning solvents.

Vises are essential. The best are manufactured specifically for holding skis, singly or in pairs. Current models can be acquired with adapters designed to hold skis that have trape-

zoidal cross sections. If you already own ski vises, adapters can be ordered from shop equipment suppliers.

If you do not have a ski vise, a basic carpenter's vise can be used as a substitute, but extra care must be taken to protect the ski from damage. Place wooden blocks between the steel jaws of the vise and the side walls of the skis. Short sections of old garden hose slit lengthwise also help protect the sidewalls of the ski. Be careful not to overtighten any vise.

You will need blocks of wood to support the tips and tails of the skis to allow you to put the necessary pressure on the tools you will be using. You will also need brake retainers, or heavy rubber bands, to secure the arms of the brake and keep them out of the way while you work.

Cleaning

Begin by wiping the ski clean (top, sides, and base) with a damp paper towel. Secure the ski in the vise. If the ski base is dirty, use a ski base cleaner to remove old wax and grit and allow time for the solvent to evaporate. This may take as long as 20 minutes. If there is grit on the bottom of an un-waxed ski, do not clean the ski with a scraper. This can force grit particles into the base material. All wax must be removed from nicks and gouges to assure a good bond when filling with P-tex. An old toothbrush is a handy tool to use.

Making Base Repairs

Minor base damage (nicks, scratches, and surface gouges) can be repaired easily with high-density P-tex. P-tex bonds well with extruded polyethylene bases and, if applied with care, offers satisfactory repairs to sintered bases. The method is an old one, but it still works well.

Choose a high-density P-tex that contains a minimal amount of paraffin. Sometimes it is possible to tell the difference in the types of P-tex by taking a P-tex stick in your fingers and bending it. Usually, the softer and more flexible the P-tex, the more paraffin it contains. The stiffer and denser it is, the better. You may also be able to tell the difference in P-tex density when removing excess P-tex with a scraper.

Serious gouges that penetrate the base and expose core materials (rubber, fiberglass, or aluminum) are best repaired by using a P-tex gun or a plastic welder or by patching. This type of repair service is routine for a ski shop but should not be attempted unless proper equipment and materials are available.

After cleaning the base, light your propane torch and hold it horizontally

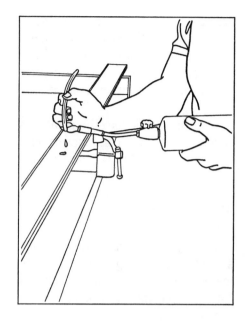

over the ski. Hold the P-tex candle in the tip of the flame until it starts to drip. The heat of the torch will keep the plastic candle from collecting carbon, which looks unsightly and can hurt the bond. If a small amount of carbon does appear, it can be removed with a scraper when the base is smoothed.

Most experienced hand tuners prefer a torch because it will enable you to get a nice bead rolling off the candle. You can work faster, and it reduces the amount of soot or carbon that forms. The flame heats the P-tex so it goes onto the ski hotter and helps produce a good bond.

If you work with a burning P-tex candle, have an ordinary paraffin candle with a wick handy so you can apply more heat to the end of the stick without having to light matches or use a lighter. One way to cut the amount of carbon that forms is to keep your P-tex candles in the freezer until you need one. The cold apparently reduces the rate at which soot collects. Another way to keep carbon from dripping onto the ski is to keep a metal scraper handy. Every time you see a piece of soot ready to flow off the candle, catch the drop on the scraper. When the candle burns clean, return to the ski.

Drip the plastic into the scratches slowly. If the P-tex continues to burn while on the ski, blow out the flame immediately. Deeper gouges may have to be passed over more than once. Allow the plastic to cool between passes.

When you have finished filling in the scratches and gouges, use a sharp metal scraper to remove excess P-tex. Make certain the scraper is sharp.

To sharpen a scraper, clamp it firmly in a vise and lay your 8-inch file lengthwise on the scraper with the tang point toward you. Pressure the file while pushing it away, keeping it as flat as you can. Some technicians prefer to place the file flat on the bench, then move the scraper over the file.

After the P-tex has cooled, with the ski in the vise, hold the scraper on the ski, place a thumb near each bottom corner of the scraper. Tilt the scraper away from you and push it down the ski, removing the excess P-tex in even sheets until you have removed the bumps and the base looks smooth.

The quickest way to finish the job is with a buffing wheel, but you can buff by hand using a sanding block with worn, fine grit paper. Do not buff too aggressively when using any abrasive on the bottom of a ski.

For deeper gouges, a P-tex gun is the most efficient tool to use. Prepare the gouge by shaving away thin sheets of base until you expose clean base material. Polyethylene applied with a P-tex gun will bond well.

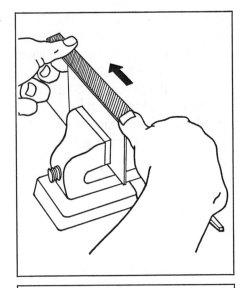

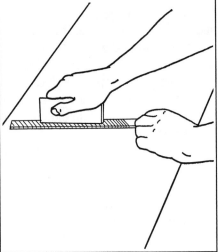

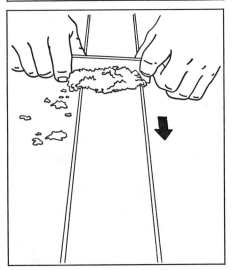

Base repairs have been complicated with the introduction of high-density sintered bases. P-tex applied hot to a clean sintered base surface will adhere satisfactorily. The key is burning in the P-tex hot.

P-tex is a much cheaper, softer grade of plastic than sintered base material. If P-tex is used, the gliding ability of the sintered base will be reduced. As P-tex is softer, it will wear down over time and may need replacing.

For the average skier, the difference in glide will not be noticeable. However, if you remove a good piece of base material along an inside edge of a good racing ski, it could affect the performance of someone trying to get to the finish line first.

In repairing recreational skis, if the gouge in a sintered base is not too deep, and if you can get a nice bead flowing from the candle, a P-tex candle will still do the job. If the gouge is too deep, a P-tex gun or hot air welder is a more suitable tool to use.

Edge Repairs

A skier who hits a rock or any other hard object with the edge of a ski may "case harden" the metal in the damaged area. In normal filing, the file will skip over the hardened area. This hardened area can be smoothed most effectively with a 10-inch Pansar file.

Work only the damaged area. One light stroke from each side, holding the file flat and parallel against the edge, will usually be enough to chip away hardened material from above the edge. A stone or silicon carbide paper wrapped around a block may also be used.

If the damage is deep (below the plane of the edge), file the edges on either side of the damaged area, but do not file below the plane of the edge. Remove as much excess material as you can, and smooth out the indentation with a fine-grade silicon carbide paper. Minor irregularities should not affect the ski's performance.

Sharpening and Adding Bevel

After the base of the ski has been cleaned and all repairs completed, check the results with a true bar before you begin working with your files. Place the true bar across the base of the ski and check every few inches, tip to tail, moving the bar the length of the ski.

Use backlighting, or lift the ski to the light, to highlight the base. This will tell you if the ski base is flat, convex, or concave or if the edges are railed. (A railed edge is an edge-high ski that, under a magnifying glass, resembles a railroad track.) You will know approximately how much filing will be necessary.

Take your 10-inch mill file and lay it across the ski at an angle with the tang end closest to you, keeping the angle between 30 and 45 degrees. As you work, you will adjust to the most effective cutting angle.

Push down on the file with about 15 to 20 pounds of pressure, stroking in comfortable lengths down the edges, tip to tail. If you feel more comfortable pulling the file toward you, stand at the tail and pull from the tip toward you. Most ski tuners find it more difficult to apply the needed downward pressure when pulling the file.

Take off the filings in smooth layers. Do not use excessive pressure, and do not try to remove too much material at once. Clean the file often with a file card or wire brush—every two or three strokes. Do not try to bend the file. Concentrate on one edge at a time. Keep filing until you cannot easily remove any more metal.

Hold the true bar across the base of the ski and look at the sliver of light coming through on each side. This sliver of light should be visible extending inward from the metal edge about an eighth to three-sixteenths of an inch. The light you see shows you the angle of bevel you have applied to the ski.

The harder new sintered bases take on a sheen near the edges which makes it easy to check on how far into the base area you have filed. Another way to check is to take a magic marker and draw lines perpendicular to the edges across the base in several spots along the length of the ski. As you wear away the lines, you can tell how far into the base material you are filing. The beveled area should be consistent from the tip to the tail for the smoothest, most predictable ride.

Today, discussions about beveling tend to concentrate more on how much to bevel rather than whether to bevel or not. Experienced ski technicians have been beveling skis for years.

The simple act of placing pressure on the ends of a file tends to shave more material off the edges and the base near the edges than from the center of the base. Applying the right amount of bevel involves some trial and error.

If you are working on your own skis, the best approach is to start with a minimal amount of bevel and go skiing. Each time you work on your skis, increase the amount of bevel until you

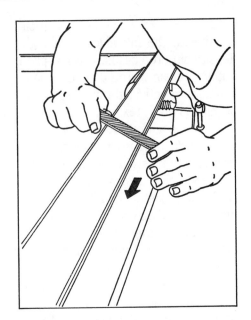

are happy with the way the skis perform. Keep in mind that most catalog or brochure illustrations that show beveling are exaggerated for effect. You do not have to remove much edge to achieve a one degree bevel.

Racers and aggressive skiers who ski with extreme angulation usually like more bevel than skiers who ski in

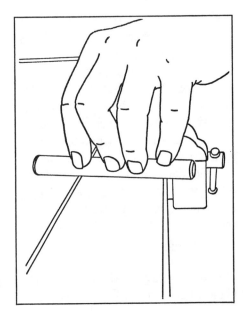

an upright position. Competition skis are usually beveled about three degrees for downhill skis, two degrees for giant slalom skis, and one degree for slalom skis. For recreational skiers skiing on hardpack or ice, a flat filed ski still works well.

Sharpening Side Edges

To file side edges, place the ski in the vise with the base away from you, using just enough pressure to hold the

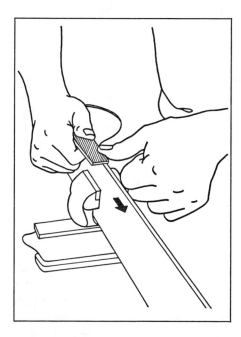

ski firmly. Use an 8-inch or 6-inch mill bastard file to work the side edges, filing from the tip to the tail while holding the file flat against the edge and parallel to the ski. The smaller files will tend to follow the contour of the ski more closely than a 10-inch or 12-inch file.

Continuous edges can be filed working from either tip or tail. Skis with cracked edges should be filed only from tip to tail.

As you shave metal off the edge, you will notice that the color changes from gray to a shiny silver. As skis have very little side edge, remove only enough material to produce a sharp edge. With the edge sharpened properly, you should be able to shave a curl off your fingernail by running it across the edge. As an alternative to using a hand-held file, inexpensive edge-sharpening tools are available which hold the file at the correct angle.

Microscopic burrs will be left on the edges after filing. Use a diamond stone, rubber stone, silicon carbide paper wrapped around a file, or an emery cloth to clean away the burrs and touch up the edge.

Detuning

Most manufacturers recommend dulling the edges from the tip to the contact point on the snow and from the contact point at the tail to the end of the ski. Taking some of the sharpness from the edge keeps the ski from "hooking." Some skiers prefer the outside edge dulled farther back from tip and tail than the inside edge.

Structuring

Perfectly smooth bases will not glide as well, particularly in warm or wet snow, as bases that have been textured or structured. Base structuring breaks the suction underneath the ski and opens the pores in the base material to improve the ability of the ski to absorb and hold wax. Structuring can be accomplished with a stone grinder or by using hand tools. The goals are the same, and good results can be obtained by either method.

Good-quality skis today are stone ground before they leave the factory. To structure by hand, you can use a riller bar or a brass brush. A riller bar, which cuts parallel grooves into the base material, is the cleanest and quickest.

Silicon carbide paper wrapped around a file also works. This is a more time-consuming process because it takes extra time to clean particles from the base material. The abrasive paper scores the base by tearing through the base material to produce the structuring effect.

Working from tip to tail, one pass over the base with a riller bar should complete the job. It may take several passes with silicon carbide paper. Start with 100 grit paper and finish the job with 150 or 180 grit paper.

Clean out loose material and open the structure lines with a brass brush. Applying pressure, use a Scotch-brite pad or Fibertex and rub the base to remove loose polyethylene "hairs" that have been raised by structuring.

Waxing

Finish the tuning job by applying a heavy coat of protective base wax. All wax manufacturers have a particular wax they recommend for impregnating newly prepared bases, but there is no universal color of wax produced for this purpose.

To seal the base, heat a waxing iron to a mid-range temperature. An old household iron adopted for the purpose should be turned to the "wool" temperature range. If the wax begins to smoke at anytime while you are waxing, the iron is too hot.

Hold the iron above the running surface of the ski, and melt wax against the bottom of the iron. Move the iron the length of the ski, allowing wax to flow in a stream onto the base as you move.

When you have finished applying wax, pass the iron over the base, melting the wax into the pores. If the skis are going to be used for skiing within a short time, remove all excess wax with a plastic scraper. Clean out the groove with a dull screwdriver, and remove any wax that remains on the side walls. Then add new wax suitable for the day's conditions.

If the skis are not going to be used soon, or are to be stored or carried in a car-top ski rack, leave the heavier coat of wax on the skis for protection.

Importance of Tuning

Whatever the successes or failures of ski tests conducted by ski publications, the most important bit of information produced by testing is that tuning and ski preparation usually have more to do with how well a ski performs than how well it was made. An average ski perfectly prepared will almost always outski a better-quality ski that has been neglected. Obviously, the goal is to put an excellent pair of skis onto the hill perfectly tuned.

Fortunately, with a bit of practice and the right tools, hand-tuning skills can be learned by anyone. The complete rejuvenation of a slightly out of tune pair of skis takes relatively little time.

Not many years ago, buying a pair of skis from a shop's retail rack was an ordeal. Pair after pair had to be inspected and selected to find matching side cuts, identical camber, similar flex, and the best base finish. The skis were then turned over to the shop's technician for a tune-up, the key ingredient to ski performance. Knowledgeable tuners miraculously gave the skis predictable gliding and turning characteristics using not easily understood tuning techniques and skills. Poor tuning, or no tuning at all, often left the skier with hooky and grabby edges, no edge control, or skis that moved like snails over the snow.

Times have changed. Ski manufacturers now know that the technology used internally to make a ski only makes a difference if the skis are properly prepared by an experienced tuner. Many ski manufacturers, realizing the importance of high quality ski finishes, have invested heavily in sophisticated machine finishing systems that provide a level of finish light years ahead of what was previously available.

Thanks to the efforts of most ski makers, only a minimal amount of tuning is usually necessary between the time skis are taken off the retail rack and when they are slope-ready (all new skis should be checked). Skis must glide well and turn predictably to offer the skier enjoyable performance.

While manufacturers have taken positive steps to deliver finely tuned skis, the effort is wasted if the skier or shop technician does not make an effort to duplicate the finish produced by the manufacturer. Temperature changes during shipping can change the core materials of skis. All new skis should be tuned when they are mounted to obtain the best possible performance.

It is relatively easy for shop technicians to duplicate the finish on models the shops sell because they are familiar with the models sold. Shop personnel asked to tune skis that they are not familiar with should take the time to check the manufacturer's technical manuals for tuning instructions. If technical manuals are not available, brand and model listings published in the September/October issue of *Ski Tech* magazine each year include the manufacturer's recommended tuning procedures.

2 Tuning with Stone Grinders

The acceptance of stone grinders as a necessary piece of shop equipment has taken place in a few short years. But despite the proven advantages of a stone grinder for tuning and maintenance, many ski shop owners still underestimate its value.

Using a wet belt sander on ski bases was the accepted industry standard for years. Then ski manufacturers began using ultra high molecular weight (UHMW) sintered polyethylenes for ski base material. This material increased base durability but at the same time made skis more difficult to finish on wet belt sanders. Although these sanders are still a valuable back shop machine, stone grinding has several advantages over wet belt sanding and hand tuning.

First, with reasonable competency on the part of the technician, there is some measure of built-in quality control for producing a flat base with a stone grinder. Second, a stone ground finish creates a fiber-free base. Belt sanding produces unwanted fiber or small hairs that are oxidized by the sun's ultraviolet rays,

making skis sluggish during gliding. Third, stone grinding can provide widely varying yet consistent base structuring.

Some stone grinding fans claim the seam found on all wet sanding belts causes variations in the texture laid into a ski base. A belt also tends to remove more base than edge, producing a railed ski. These problems can be minimized by a well-designed belt sander, but, properly used, a stone grinder always gives a flatter, cleaner finish.

With a stone grinder, it is possible to get a fast, completely mechanical tune-up, and a good mechanic can do as many as 10 base jobs an hour using a good machine. It is difficult to compete today in retail ski sales and service without a stone grinder.

Product literature distributed by the manufacturers, most of whom also produce belt sanders, adds a few other reasons that stone grinders are a necessary tool for the well-equipped service department. Stone grinding enables the proficient ski technician to produce base and edge quality that was simply not possible before. You can see and feel the difference. The end results are increased profits (as much as five times more cash per hour), the best possible performance from every ski, increased retail ski sales, and satisfied customers who keep coming back.

Brochure hype aside, most shop owners who use stone grinders tend to agree with the manufacturers' assessment. However, some disagreement still remains over whether a stone grinder can turn out a properly tuned ski without any hand finishing.

Still, most recreational skiers say their skis turn easier, glide better, and feel lighter after being stone ground. Better skiers and racers notice their skis are faster and smoother. The clean cut of the stone—almost like a razor blade—leaves the sintered base wide open and free to absorb more wax.

The stone grinder is not a miracle tool that can handle all ski tuning needs. It will, however, meet all your ski base finishing needs. The belt sander is still best for doing rough, preliminary work and for preparing the base for the finest finish possible with a stone grinder.

The process of stone grinding was first used commercially in 1965 by Fischer Skis in their factory at Ried, Austria. Shortly after Fischer adopted the stone grinder, Volkl also began producing skis with stone ground finishes.

During the 1980-81 season, Montana Sport, a Swiss company that produces a wide range of ski service and maintenance equipment, introduced stone grinding at the retail level in the United States. Racer service quickly adopted stone grinding, but the general skiing public and retail service de-partments were slow to follow. Wintersteiger, which uses its factory capacity to build farm implements as well as ski service equipment, shares the largest chunk of the stone grinding market worldwide with Montana Sport.

Among racers, stone ground bases are standard. Technicians preparing racing skis need to alter base structures quickly as snow conditions change, and they have to be able to reproduce a specific base texture that they know, by experience, has proven successful in similar snow conditions.

With racers using stone grinding, word slowly began to spread about its advantages. By 1983, ski factories that included stone grinding in their production process began to actively promote the fact to retailers and customers.

One reason that it was difficult for stone grinding to gain wide acceptance was service department personnel did not take the time to learn how to use the machines correctly. Stone grinders are complex machines and are more expensive than belt sanders. It takes longer to learn how to use them properly.

Every technician who plans to use a stone grinder must attend a clinic or workshop for training or take the time to gain a thorough understanding of the machine's operational manuals. It is critical that the technician follow a prescribed machine maintenance plan and make periodic checks for flatness, freedom from fiber, and proper structure. It is important that at least one technician in a shop learn how to operate the equipment properly so he or she can train others. If the first operator does not get it right, you end up with one person teaching everyone else how to do it wrong.

One of the early problems associated with stone grinders was hardened edges. Stone grinding produces considerable heat. It is important to avoid applying excessive pressure against the stone by trying to remove too much base material in one pass. Maintaining a constant flow of water over the cutting surface is vital.

Most manufacturers recommend using stone grinders only for buffing the base and creating a desired structure. If they are used as a planing device to remove excess base material, you may get hardened edges or edges ground away to nothing.

Good stone grinders come with variable speed stones and drive motors, integrated automatic feed, high-volume water cleaning and cooling systems, and a precise diamond dressing system. The diamond dresser is what keeps the stone clean and "fresh." In some models, it can be programmed to produce a specific pattern on the stone that can be duplicated on the ski base. The autofeed is an especially critical feature because it is almost impossible to reproduce a specific structure from ski to ski or obtain a consistent base on a single ski by hand feeding.

When deciding between single speed or variable speed drives, or stone speeds and dressing systems, the stone speed and dressing system is something to consider. You pay more for variable options, but they provide more precise operator control. Preset or fixed speeds make for a simpler operation.

One option the service department can choose from is whether to buy a combination wet belt/stone grinder or stand-alone units. The choice usually depends on the volume of business the shop does. If the shop expects a heavy business in complete ski tune-ups, the stand-alone unit may be the best choice. Such machines offer the capability to set up "assembly line" finishing—like that found in ski factories. Many of the combination models function only in a stone or wet belt mode.

Most producers and distributors of stone grinders say they are just starting to tap the real market potential for their machines. The demand for machine finishing, including complex structuring, is now just the tip of the iceberg. Customer demand in the United States will grow rapidly for this level of service and expertise just as it has in Europe.

3 *Base Options*

With the creation of clear sintered bases and carbon/graphite sintered bases, the options available to ski manufacturers multiplied. Not many years ago, ski makers were limited only to variations of extruded polyethylene.

By now, most ski technicians understand the basic difference between extruded and sintered bases. But a more detailed examination of base material characteristics will help explain how those differences affect tuning and performance. It is best to remember, however, that while the new ultra high molecular weight (UHMW) sintered polyethylene bases have contributed to improved ski performance, they contribute less than good design and construction, base structure treatment, and waxing.

Two major advantages that sintered bases have over extruded bases are a greater ability to absorb wax and a greater ability to resist damage. Almost all sintered bases used today have a molecular weight (MW) in the realm of 3.5 million. It is possible to produce sintered bases with a higher molecular weight, but those bases become more difficult to grind or repair. And design parameters for maximum performance may not require a higher molecular weight base.

It is possible to make a slightly harder sintered base through molecular cross-linking. The result of a modified 3.5 million MW base is a base that should perform slightly better in cold fresh snow when humidity is low. The material can be cross-linked in clear or "black." Its higher cost and limited availability would restrict its use to skis being produced by a manufacturer's race department for top level racers.

The sintered polyethylene material currently used was originally developed for the mining industry. There was a need for a high-resistance material with optimum sliding properties that would not change with low temperatures. Today, sintered polyethylene is used to line chutes, bunkers, and troughs and to line dump truck beds and other equipment that carry damp or muddy materials. Ski manufacturing is a secondary market.

Extruded bases range from about 200,000 to 500,000 MW. Generally, the higher the molecular weight, the lower the density. It is the lower density of sintered bases that allows for higher wax absorption. As a result of heat, pressure, and time, sintered base molecules combine to form crystals. And as the sintering process continues, the crystals combine to form grains.

Areas that are noncrystalline are low in density. This creates a base material consisting of crystalline areas, called grains, and amorphous areas, the gap between the grains. The amorphous area is not molecularly fixed. It expands with heat and contracts with cold. This is why wax absorption increases when wax is ironed on hot.

Extruded polyethylene base material is pressed together in a more consistent form. There are no separate crystalline or noncrystalline areas.

With the development of carbon/graphite bases, it became possible to photograph the base material so the pattern of crystalline and amorphous areas was visible. The distinction was not as apparent when photographing clear sintered base material.

Sintered bases have 1.5 to 2 percent air porosity. There are two pore sizes. Micro is about 200-250 Angstroms in size, and macro is about 2,000 to 3,000 Angstroms in size. (An Angstrom is one ten-millionth of a millimeter.)

When wax is applied to sintered bases with heat, five or six milligrams of wax can be absorbed per square centimeter. Extruded base materials absorb only 1 to 1.5 milligrams per square centimeter. When ironing on wax, the temperature should be kept in the range of 212 to 248 degrees Fahrenheit, or 100 to 120 degrees Celsius. Skis are manufactured with ski press temperatures of about 150 degrees C, the approximate temperature needed to release the resins used to bond the core materials. High waxing temperatures approaching or above those used in the manufacturing process may damage the skis.

Cross-country skis should be waxed using a temperature of about 100 degrees C; alpine skis require about 120 degrees C.

Heat applied over a period of time increases the amount of wax that is absorbed. Two or three minutes of ironing at 120 degrees C approaches maximum absorption per square centimeter. Beyond that, the additional amount of absorption falls off rapidly.

Waxing irons designed specifically for applying wax usually have temperature dials to control heat. Temperatures may be somewhat below that indicated on the dial when the iron is used because the ski will pull heat out of the iron, but the actual temperatures are reasonably accurate.

If you are using a household iron for waxing, it is possible to determine the iron's surface temperature using Tempilstiks, temperature-indicating crayons available at any store that sells welding supplies. For example, buy a Tempilstik that melts at 100 degrees C. Hold the stick against the surface of the iron while slowly increasing the temperature setting. When the crayon begins to melt, check the setting. If it says "linen" or "cotton," you know that specific setting produces a surface temperature of 100 degrees.

While there is general agreement that sintered base materials are superior to extruded bases, there is no consensus as to whether carbon/graphite, or "black" bases, are superior to clear sintered bases. Experience gained during a number of racing seasons will help determine the answer, as it takes several seasons of testing and racing for patterns to emerge.

Early tests seem to indicate that the skiing environment plays an important role in performance of the carbon/graphite base. The lower the humidity, the greater the performance dropoff. But unless race results show carbon/graphite bases have a distinct advantage over clear bases, it is unlikely ski manufacturers will continue to use all-black bases and give up the opportunity to display their name and logo on the bottoms of the skis.

If there is a decrease in the use of carbon/graphite bases on racing skis, there probably will be an increase in the use of carbon/graphite on high-performance recreational skis. At the recreational level, the primary advantage of a carbon/graphite base is appearance. It has proven to be a good base with low friction characteristics. Dirt, scratches, or patches do not show as readily as they do on clear bases. Theoretically, the carbon/graphite base may prove to be most suitable for cross-country skis, as it works well on moist, dirty snow.

The percentage of carbon/graphite being used in ski bases ranges from 1 to 7.5 percent. Percentages higher than the latter are impractical; there is reduced resistance to tearing, making the base difficult to grind. In grinding, sanding, or waxing, carbon/graphite and clear sintered bases are treated the same.

4 *Base Material Glossary*

ew and improved ways of using synthetic materials in manufacturing ski equipment have contributed greatly to product durability and performance. It is not always necessary to understand how a product is made, but it is necessary to learn how to take care of it to obtain maximum performance.

The definitions below help explain the technical differences in base materials used in producing skis today.

Base Wax: An all-purpose sealer wax used to impregnate base materials. Base wax should be applied as the final step in tuning. It protects the base and provides a foundation for applying running waxes for current conditions.

Beveling: Produces a slightly convex running surface by filing one to three degrees of "bevel" extending an eighth to a quarter of an inch onto the edge and running surface. Beveling may also be applied using a stone grinder.

Concave: Base worn more in the center than at the edges, which makes it difficult to initiate a turn. Similar to railing. A concave ski is easily

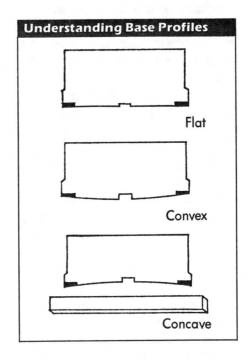

Understanding Base Profiles

Flat

Convex

Concave

identified when checked using a true bar. Light will be visible under the bar between the two edges.

Convex: Base material in the center of the ski is higher than the edges. A slightly convex ski is easy to get into a turn. A ski too convex will tend to wander.

Case Harden: When an edge strikes a rock or other hard material, the sudden compression of the metal edge hardens the metal. The "case-hardened" spot can be harder than a metal file and must be smoothed out with a stone.

Density: The ratio between weight and volume of base materials.

Extruded Base: Two different basic manufacturing processes are used to produce base materials found on all current model skis—extruded and sintered polyethylene. To produce extruded base materials, polyethylene is heated until it is molten and forced through a die into the dimensions to be used for ski bases. Extruded polyethylene has a relatively high density and low molecular weight. Extruded polyethylene base material is the easiest to repair, but it is less resistant to wear than sintered polyethylene and does not absorb wax as well.

Sintered Base: To produce sintered base materials, polyethylene powder is heated slowly under heavy pressure until the particles melt and bond together. The material is compressed into a round disk approximately 4 inches thick and 3.5 feet in diameter. After the compressed polyethylene has cooled, it is shaved in a continuous sheet to provide base material of the right thickness and width for ski manufacturing.

Sintered Base (Clear): This is base material with a molecular weight of 3.5 million produced from polyethylene powder with no additional additives.

Sintered Base (Carbon/Graphite): From 1 to 7.5 percent carbon/graphite is added to polyethylene powder to produce a sintered black base material believed to have better performance characteristics on wet snow under conditions of high humidity. Carbon/graphite added above 7.5 percent reduces the resistance of the base to tearing and the base becomes difficult to grind. Of the 7.5 percent, not more than 2 percent is carbon.

Sintered Base Composition: Sintered base materials consist of crystalline and amorphous areas (see below).

Crystalline Areas: In producing sintered bases, as a result of heat, pressure, and time, molecules are combined to form crystals and crystalline areas. The crystalline areas are hard, with high density and little molecular movement.

Amorphous Areas: These are the gaps between crystalline areas which have the potential of absorbing wax. These areas are less dense, there is more freedom of molecular movement, and the material is less hard.

Crystallinity: The ratio between amorphous and crystalline areas in percentages.

Offset Edge: Steel edges offset from side walls of skis to make it possible to file or sharpen the vertical edge to a 90 degree angle or to apply a bevel.

Railed Edges: Similar to convex. Often, obviously railed skis are caused by shrinkage of the base material or careless use of abrasives when tuning which cause the polyethylene to wear faster than the steel edges. In tuning a ski with railed edges, particularly machine tuning, care must be taken not to work too rapidly and to overheat or case harden the edges.

Stone Grinding: The "stone" used in stone grinding is similar to the wheel of a bench grinder. This important tool is considered to be the best machine method of producing a relatively fiber-free and flat base. The stone, trued with a diamond dressing tool, has the ability to cut through base and metal edge material equally. Stone grinders can be used to structure (apply a texture pattern) the base. By varying the type of dressing tool used, the speed at which the ski is fed through the machine and the pressure applied make it possible to produce a variety of structure patterns.

Structure: The friction of skis sliding over snow melts snow crystals and produces a fine film of water under the base of the ski. By applying a texture to the bottom of the ski, the uneven surface breaks the suction or drag and permits the ski to glide freely by increasing the airflow between the ski and the snow. Structuring can be accomplished with a stone grinder or by hand using a riller bar, brass brush, or abrasive papers.

5 *The Basic Hand File*

The basic file is still the essential tool a great ski technician must master. But tools are only as good as the mechanic using them. It takes many tune-ups to develop a good tool sense and a feel for the tools you are using. To use a file properly, you need to practice until every stroke is efficient and smooth.

If you are a beginning ski tuner, or if you simply want to brush up, these are the essential steps to take to turn out skis properly beveled. Start by collecting a set of 8-, 10-, and 12-inch mill bastard files. Six-inch and 14-inch files are optional. Individual skiers who are experienced in tuning their own skis usually prefer using the shorter length files. Technicians who turn out a high volume of hand-tuned skis usually work with longer files as they are more efficient and accelerate the work.

Beginning ski tuners should start with a 10-inch file. It is easy to handle and will help the beginner produce cleaner work with less chance of error.

You will notice that the teeth on the 8-inch file are closer together than the teeth on the 12-inch file, if the files are of the same brand. This may not be true when mixing brands of files. Also notice how much thinner the profile is on the 8-inch file and how the files get thicker proportionally as they get longer.

Take the 8-inch file in both hands and try to bend it. You will see the steel bow slightly. Try this with each of the files. See how the longer ones are more difficult to bend—if you can bend them at all.

You can see why pushing a shorter, smaller file down the length of the ski will give you a larger degree of bevel than a longer, less flexible file. Shorter, more flexible files produce the greatest bevel and stiff, longer files the least.

The steps that follow demonstrate the uses of the different length files. First, lock an old ski (one you are not afraid to damage) into a vise. If there is any excess wax or grime on the base, use a plastic scraper to clean the bottom of the ski. If you have difficulty, you can finish the job with a base cleaner.

Take a stone and deburr the edges if they are not clean. If you have a true bar, this is a good time to check the base so you will have a better idea of the condition of the ski. Take the 12-inch file and, with the tang or pointed end angled toward you, push the file down the ski with little or no pressure. If you are drawing the file toward you, the tang will be angled away. The tang is always pointed away from the cutting direction. Look at the file. See any edge filings? Probably not.

Now file with heavy pressure, 20 to 25 pounds or more. You will be able to feel that the file is not working smoothly. It will grab and skip across the ski. The correct amount of pressure obviously lies somewhere in between. Fifteen pounds is about the maximum amount of pressure you should use. Start out with light pressure and increase the pressure throughout the stroke, then lighten up. If you start out with maximum pressure, you are likely to create chatter. It is not necessary to be exact. If you are working on a ski that is already beveled, you will have to apply more pressure to remove any steel.

If you practice using the file with even, comfortable strokes, you will begin to apply the right amount of pressure. The goal is to remove steel from the edges in even layers, not all at once. If you are working properly, you will also be including a bit of the base in the bevel.

For many ski tuners, pushing the file instead of pulling or drawing it works best. The shoulders are over the work and the strokes are right for the length of the arms, not too short and not too long.

Other experienced ski tuners prefer pulling the file toward the body, finishing the stroke in a position that gives the tuner a stable platform. Because it is harder to pressure a file while pulling it, technicians who use this method usually use a smaller file, 6 or 8 inches instead of 10 inches. The key is to choose the method that feels the most comfortable.

Start at the tip of the ski and file a section until it is smooth and even. Then continue working down the ski toward the tail filing in overlapping sections. Never overwork one section, but keep feathering one section into the next.

The edge should be smooth and even throughout. Many ski tuners find that by flipping the ski in the vise (swinging the tip around to point in the opposite direction), they can shave a little more steel because one arm may be stronger than the other.

The angle of the file across the ski is also important. If you hold the file at too great an angle, the filings may scratch the base and the steel edge. It will remove steel in "chunks" instead of "sheets." If you hold the file at too small an angle, you will not remove much steel, and it will take many more strokes than necessary. This can heat and temper the steel. The proper angle is about 25 degrees, but there is a range of angles, plus or minus a few degrees, that will enable you to work efficiently. The actual angle of the teeth of the file may vary slightly from brand to brand.

Experienced ski tuners will change the angle slightly as they work and move the file so that it cuts over the full surface. This uses all the elements of the teeth, makes the file last longer, and is the most efficient. You can get the feel for the range of angle that does the most even and efficient job.

Always keep the file clean by brushing away the filings after every eight to ten strokes. A combination wire and fibered file card works well. Usually, the fiber side is enough to remove metal filings without dulling the file. The wire side is useful for removing plastic that may gum up the file's teeth.

After filing sections, run over the full length of the base with the 12-inch file. When your file glides evenly, section by section, from tip to tail, and more metal is difficult to remove, check your work with a true bar. You should see a slight bevel that runs across the edge and about 1/8-inch into the plastic base.

Next, put the ski back in the vise and try experimenting with the 10-inch file. You will find you have to determine the proper pressure all over again because this file is thinner and bows more. With each file, you should use just enough pressure to allow the file to remove steel in clean, even layers.

Make efficient, smooth strokes down the ski and you will see more steel coming off than you removed with the 12-inch file. When finished, look at your work with a true bar. The angle of bevel should be slightly greater than it was with the 12-inch file.

Go through the same steps with the 8-inch file, which will require the lightest pressure of all. When you check using the true bar, you will see that you have added the largest bevel yet.

As you improve your filing skills, you can concentrate on one edge at a time as long as you keep the file flat across the ski and avoid rocking it up off either edge. If you try putting a flat stick or a washer under one side of the file, it is much more difficult to get the file to work efficiently. The bevel that results is usually too great. All you really need to do is apply the proper pressure to the correct length file and use it until edge filings can no longer be removed easily.

A 10-inch or 12-inch file will usually produce a small bevel appropriate for most recreational skiers. The 8-inch and 6-inch files are generally used on racing skis, although a smaller bevel may make the ski hold better in icy conditions. When you are finished filing, use a stone or wrap silicon carbide paper around the file to smooth out any irregularities and polish the edges.

When beginning to work on your own skis, start out by applying a minimum amount of bevel—no more than a half to one degree. As you have an opportunity to use the skis, increase the amount of bevel until you feel the ski is performing the way you want it to. Then back off and continue preparing your skis with approximately that same amount of bevel. It is easier to add more bevel than take it away.

After you have become proficient with your files, you will be able to shape the ski any way you wish. The file will help you feel the high spots and the low spots so you can even them out. You will prove the value of your work when you take a perfectly prepared pair of skis out for a run.

Skiers who want to be able to touch up their skis while they are traveling can carry a few essential items of tuning equipment that will take care of most basic tuning jobs.

One or two files (a 6-inch and 8-inch file can do the work), a whetstone (one that can be carried in your pocket while skiing), some rub-on wax, Scotch-brite, a plastic scraper, a small nylon brush, and some emery paper (about 220 grit) will take care of the basics. This makes a small enough package to fit into a ski pack.

How much tuning equipment you decide to carry will depend largely on whether you are driving and can carry a tool box in the trunk of your car or are flying and want to limit what you take along. If you have room, a portable iron can come in handy.

6 *Beveling Bases*

Over a period of years, beveling ski bases for better performance has evolved from an unconscious act to a conscious decision. Experienced ski technicians working with files to "flat file" a pair of skis have always applied some bevel simply through pressure applied to the ends of the file while filing. The pressure puts a slight bow in the file to produce a slightly convex base.

When at one time a bevel might have been applied almost by accident, today, ski tuners take extra care to apply the degree of bevel best suited to the flex of the ski, the ability of the skier, and the snow conditions. Skis should not be base-edge beveled every time they are sharpened, however. Think of the edge as having two planes, the base edge and the side edge. A crisp edge can be maintained between base beveling by sharpening the side edge of the skis.

Since skiers have become conscious of beveling, there have been a number of methods suggested for applying bevel while tuning skis by hand—some of questionable merit. One suggestion has been to take a wrap or two of duct tape or masking tape around one end of the file so the tape lifts the file off one edge of the ski and files the opposite edge at an angle. Another method has been described as the "popsicle stick" method. A flat stick or washer is slipped under one end of the file to create an angle for the file shaving the opposite edge.

There are also a number of hand beveling tools on the market today. Most beveling tools are adjustable, which makes it possible to come close to achieving the exact degree of bevel desired. These tools are portable and are particularly handy for individual skiers to use for minor tuning and touch-up when on ski trips. They are not practical for high volume shop use. While there are advocates for each method of adding bevel (and it makes sense to experiment and use the method that works best for you), most experienced ski technicians recommend working primarily with a good set of files and applying bevel the old-fashioned way.

Some tuning experts recommend beveling without using any aids be-

Edge Sharpening Options

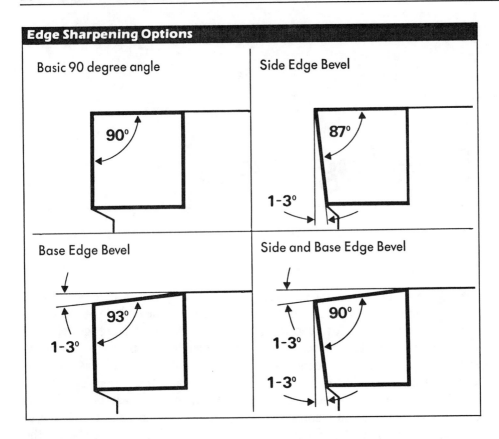

Basic 90 degree angle — 90°

Side Edge Bevel — 87°, 1-3°

Base Edge Bevel — 93°, 1-3°

Side and Base Edge Bevel — 90°, 1-3°, 1-3°

cause they believe using tape can apply too much of an angle and too much bevel. If you take about equal amounts of edge and base when beveling, the end result should be a ski with a slightly convex, contoured profile with no noticeable angle at the point where the bevel stops and the flat ski begins.

Most technical drawings produced for technical manuals or tuning books show an exaggerated angle of bevel simply because a one-, two-, or even three-degree angle is almost imperceptible—one or two hundredths of an inch from square. While there are tools available to measure the degree of bevel, it is almost impossible to consciously plan for, say, a two-degree bevel on a pair of skis. It is mostly a matter of touch, feel, and experience —learning to relax and be comfortable using your files.

After you have finished filing a pair of skis, use a true bar to check the amount of bevel. The space between the true bar and the edge should not be as much as the thickness of a cardboard matchbook cover, and it should be slightly more than the thickness of a good piece of letterhead.

A good technician uses only basic files to apply bevel, usually finishing off the work with a 6-inch mill bastard file. Technicians traveling the World Cup circuit carry 10-, 8-, and 6-inch mill bastard files in the toolbox along with body files to take care of serious rock damage and for working with brand-new skis. The other key ingredients are whetstones, stones, sandpaper, nylon and metal brushes, and plastic scrapers.

The most common file selections carried for hand tuning are 8-, 10-, and 12-inch mill bastard files. But a 6-inch file gives a fine finish to a well-prepared pair of skis.

There are a lot of factors to be considered when trying to decide on the right bevel. The most important consideration is the ski and skier combination. If you have a novice skier on a pair of high performance skis, you bevel more than normal to take some of the zip out of a ski that can overpower the novice. Snow conditions are another factor. Harder snow requires more edge.

The base edge is beveled for turnability and glide and the side edge for grip. Three degrees are pretty extreme on the base edge while 1/2 to 1 degree is average. Some manufacturers today are producing skis with 1/2 to 1 degree of bevel on the skis they deliver.

Machine edgers may vary the actual bevel slightly from what you believe you are getting, but the difference is unnoticeable to most novices. For racers, especially downhillers and Super G skiers, the effects are noticeable. Since a lot of turning is not required in downhill, you bevel to get the edge off the snow altogether because the edge does create drag and friction.

The increasing use of dampening materials in skis means the edge of the ski is in direct contact with the snow for a much greater percentage of the time. This accentuates the pluses or minuses of a proper bevel.

Some technicians prefer using a hand beveler rather than a file for race tune-ups because they believe it offers greater precision. For machine tuning, some wet belt sanders, as well as some stone grinders, turn out skis with a bevel that is perfectly adequate for recreational ski beveling.

Most technicians agree that a good ski technician working with files can turn out a perfectly prepared pair of skis. Some technicians use a wrap or two of masking tape around the file for beveling. The problem with wrapping tape on one end is that the bevel will not extend 1/8-inch to 3/16-inch into the base material. It causes the file to bevel only the outer half of the metal edge. There are some technicians who are good with their hands and can feel the amount of bevel they are putting on the ski, but using tape can serve as a guide for an inexperienced ski tuner. One degree of bevel in the base is about normal. The one degree norm was arrived at through trial and error and feedback.

Man-made snow tends to be a little icy. So skis that are to be used on man-made snow should be somewhat forgiving. One of the variables is how far toward the tip and tail the bevel is extended. Some skiers want the ski to come into the turn easily, while others want the ski to really bite into the turn. Generally, for beginning and novice skiers, bevel far forward and backward so the ski eases into the turn by providing 2 to 2-1/2 degrees of tip and tail bevel. To achieve a biting bevel for more advanced skiers, provide a 1- to 2-degree bevel at the tip and the tail. At the center of the ski, decrease it so the ski is flatter underfoot. Many skiers like an even bevel from tip to tail for predictability.

While there may be some disagreement as to how much bevel to apply, the ultimate test is how well the ski performs. The proper bevel is still determined by a combination of the flex of the ski, the skier's ability, and the snow conditions.

If you are working on your own skis, you can experiment by applying a minimal amount of bevel, skiing on the skis, then increasing the amount of bevel every time you tune your skis. By experimenting, you will eventually arrive at a pair of skis beveled to a degree that works best for you. Applying bevel involves some trial and error.

In beveling skis for others, a flat filed ski with a minimum bevel still works best for recreational skiers skiing on hard pack or ice. Racers and aggressive skiers who ski with extreme angulation usually like more bevel than skiers who ski in an upright stance. Through experimentation, competition skis usually perform best if the downhill ski has the greatest bevel, the giant slalom ski less, and the slalom ski the lightest.

In preparing a downhill ski, the bevel in the shovel area may have three degrees, the forebody may have two degrees, and under the foot just one. Then that is reversed working toward the tail of the ski. This may vary, but the downhill ski will have more of a bevel than the giant slalom ski.

There are a couple of ways you can check the bevel, depending on the color of the base. Sometimes it is easier to see on a black or dark-colored base. If you have a nice pattern in the base from a stone grinder or a belt, by passing the file over it, you are going to see how far it is cutting into the base. For many, it is more of a feel. Working from the tip, try making two extra passes at the tip, one in the shovel, normal over the binding area, one behind the binding, and two extra passes at the tail.

7 Answers to the Most Common Tuning Questions

Ski technicians who conduct clinics and work with shop technicians are asked many questions, some of which are asked more frequently than others. Based on the experience of Jim Deines, who has taught workshop classes since 1982, here are the questions asked most. They are the same questions the typical ski mechanic working in a shop, or the serious skier who works on his or her own equipment, would ask if given the opportunity.

1. What is beveling and how much should a ski be beveled when it is tuned?

For years, racers have been using a tuning technique called beveling, which is simply tuning ski edges at angles. Today, beveling is popular not only among racers but in most ski service shops and among many ski manufacturers who apply bevel to the bases of their new ski models before they are shipped from the factory.

Beveling a ski's edges can have a very strong effect on the performance of that ski. Often, "beveling" refers to base edge beveling. But one should be aware that the side edge can also be beveled.

Base edge beveling from a range of approximately one half to two degrees can improve the turnability and glide of the ski. More than two degrees can make a ski difficult to get on edge.

A side edge bevel range from one to four degrees will improve the grip and turning power of the edges. This can be a little difficult to do unless special tools are used.

In answer to the question, "how much?" many factors must be considered—the snow conditions, what type of skier is involved, what kind of ski is being used, and skiing speeds.

Remember, in general, a little goes a long way in beveling. It is always easier to take a little more off than put some back on. So, go easy, whether you use a file with some sort of shim (a special beveling tool with degree indicators) or a machine beveler. Most important, try to keep the bevel consistent from tip to tail. This lends itself to the smoothest carved turn possible.

2. What is the best way to repair sintered ski bases?

A sintered ski base is one of those good news/bad news stories. The good news is that it glides much better than the older, softer bases. It is also much more durable. Since it is harder to damage, it does not need to be repaired as often.

The bad news is that the repairs take a little more effort than the old drip candle repair method. You may have already discovered, in many instances, drip candle repairs have difficulty bonding to the sintered base and may fall out after only one day of skiing.

For that reason, many repair benches in ski shops and ski rooms now use all polyethylene ski repair guns called extruders. These use special repair materials that produce harder, longer-lasting repairs. They have heating nozzles that bond the repair materials and the ski base together.

You really do not need expensive extruders, even for sintered bases. If you burn the P-tex in with a torch, the hot temperature will create a bond that will last, unless the gouge in the ski is very deep.

While some of the more fully featured tools may be rather expensive, less expensive models are available for as little as $50 to $100. They are well worth the investment.

3. Do skis need a groove?

This is always an interesting question, usually revolving around the idea of need versus want versus perception. The groove in many new ski models has become shallower over the years. In some models, it has been eliminated altogether. In older skis, the deeper grooves probably provided some tracking stability.

Today, most of the stability is built into the ski by virtue of some of the space-age materials. The groove is not as important. A groove may help break up suction in wet spring snow but so will a properly prepared ski base.

The groove is part of the base profile. As the ski is tuned, scraped, sanded, and stone ground, sooner or later the groove will begin to disappear. Some shops have the ability, with tools designed specifically for this purpose, to regroove a ski. But caution is needed not to cut too deeply through the ski base when regrooving. It is better to have it too shallow than too deep.

While my guess is that most skiers could not tell the difference if their skis had a groove or not, base damage in a groove should be repaired since it will affect the ski's gliding ability.

4. Can a bent ski be repaired?

When customers come into one of our shops with a bent ski, we usually tell them we can try and rebend it, rather than straighten it. There is more than just a semantic difference here.

If a ski is bent, it has been acted on by a flexing or counterflexing force greater than its construction was designed to withstand. Consequently, it was not able to return to its normal position following the loading/unloading. By rebending the ski, the idea is basically to do it all again but in the opposite direction. Often, this can be done successfully by a skilled technician who takes care not to work too quickly and who uses moderate heat to aid the bending process.

Rebending a ski is often a "quick-fix" remedy to make a ski skiable again. Sometimes these repairs last a long time. Other times, they are only good until the ski is put under a moderate load again. Ski construction materials, as well as the severity of the bend, can dictate the longevity of repair.

Fortunately, most ski makers have the ability to "remate" a bent ski with a good one of similar flex and camber for a moderate charge. This may be a last resort effort and, with shipping and turnaround time, could involve a couple of weeks. But it is an excellent way to get back out on that favorite old pair of boards.

5. What is an Electra base?

P-tex Electra was developed and patented by IMS, the Swiss ski base manufacturer, in 1981. Shortly thereafter, it began to receive considerable attention on the racing circuits. Now, virtually every ski manufacturer uses P-tex Electra on some of their new ski models.

The basis for Electra development was P-tex 2000, an extra high molecular weight sintered polyethylene. Carbon/graphite was added to this formula for a distinct purpose—to improve the gliding properties of ski base materials.

This is done in two different ways:

(1) Unlike other conventional ski base materials, P-tex Electra is permanently antistatic because the carbon/graphite additives make the polyethylene base electrically conductive. This keeps dirt and other impurities in the snow from clinging to the base and thereby increasing drag on the ski and decreasing its good gliding ability. This characteristic works especially well in cold, dry snow.

(2) Because of the carbon/graphite additives, P-tex Electra also conducts heat better than other ski bases. This is important in warm snow and slush where there is abundant water between the ski and snow surface. Because P-tex Electra enjoys improved heat distribution, the formation of additional water is reduced and the "suction effect" common in warm moist snow is minimized.

P-tex Electra is also available on many cross-country skis as well as alpine skis. It is used extensively on racing circuits and provides optimum gliding properties over a broad range of snow conditions.

6. What is better, hand tuning or machine tuning?

This is an unfair question because it implies that one method is better than another. We prefer to think in terms of quality. There are well-tuned skis—and then there is everything else. I have seen technicians ruin skis with 10-inch mill bastard files just as quickly as others using wet belt sanding machines or stone grinders.

A tune-up done with hand tools or by machine will only be as good as "the nut on the handle," that is, the technician doing the work. One thing can be said: machines save time and can lend themselves to consistent results. But that is only if they are operated properly. A well-tuned ski done by hand usually requires more time than one done by machine. Adequate skill is required to do either.

7. Are all waxes created equal?

All ski wax manufacturers will tell you that they produce the best waxes. By and large, some may be better or worse than others—if small increments of time are important in measuring the success of your ski day. On a race course, for example, small increments do count.

Waxes for racing are usually designed for very specific temperature ranges and snow conditions. Universal, or all-purpose, waxes are developed to cover broad temperature ranges.

Wax comes in bars, buckets, cakes, chips, sprays, ointments, liquids, and impregnated towelettes. Wax can be rubbed, buffed, sprayed, wiped, brushed, machined, or ironed onto the ski base.

Chemists from the ski base manufacturers tell us that the sintered ski bases have the ability to "hold and store" wax for moderate periods because they are crystalline in construction. The best adhesion between the wax and ski is obtained when the polyethylene and wax are heated simultaneously, as when ironed.

It is most important to wax regularly. For best results, skis should be waxed every time they are used. Every other time is second best. Waxing will help you protect the ski base, as well as improve performance, by allowing the ski to glide and turn more easily.

8. When is a ski beyond repair?

One of our shop's mottos is, "If we cannot fix it, you should throw it away." We are willing to tackle just about any type of repair job (delaminations, tip and tail protector replacements, base patches, edge section repairs, complete new bases, side wall repairs) in an effort to get the skis skiable again.

However, when the core has been broken, a primary structural component is damaged "beyond repair." We will normally try to encourage the customer to look for a new pair of skis or possibly return the pair to the manufacturer. For a nominal charge, the manufacturer will remate the good ski with a used ski with similar flex and camber characteristics.

9. How far back should the ski edges be dulled?

There are a lot of different opinions when it comes to dulling ski edges. Only a few years ago, I recall watching technicians dulling edges on skis halfway from the tip to the binding toe piece on skis they had just spent an hour to get flat and sharp. They called it detuning.

Used in this manner, dulling was seemingly a predecessor to beveling. It was used by many shops to make a ski more predictable in turn initiation. The unfortunate part of abusively dulling the steel edges on the running surface is that it can take away from edge control—the carving or turning power of the skis.

Dulling ahead of and behind the running surface is good. The edge can be rounded in these areas to protect the top cosmetics of the ski as well as eliminate the "hookiness" of a ski in chopped snow conditions or in ruts on a race course. Light dulling or detuning (I prefer to call it fine tuning) of the running surface edge should only be done in the first few inches back from the shovel, providing the base edges have been properly beveled. In many cases, this fine tuning merely provides a transition between a dulled shovel and an edge with an extreme side edge bevel.

Skis tuned in this fashion are easy to initiate into turns and still have the edge control necessary for carving and turning. There are some great "rubberized" tuning stones to do this with, since only a slight keenness is taken off the edge. You never can tell when you might want to get an edge sharp again.

10. What can be done to take care of ski tops?

Service on ski tops is something I think is usually best left to the ski manufacturers. Most manufacturers offer retopping of their most popular models. Summertime is an excellent time to send them in, since retopping usually takes a bit longer than other types of service.

Trying to do spot repairs on ski tops, other than simple delaminations, often results in some "less than perfect" repairs—cosmetically speaking.

Short of doing some of these out of necessity, there are some excellent preventive steps that can be taken. The first thing is to check the top edges of a pair of skis to make sure that they have been well beveled, or rounded. This will prevent much of the top chipping if the skis "click" together when skiing. If they are not very well beveled, use a file to put some additional profile on them.

It can be advantageous, especially if you are trying to keep the cosmetics of your skis in top shape, to use one of the best coating tapes available. This protective film can go a long way in helping to minimize top surface scratches, and it can be replaced if it eventually begins to peel or fade.

PART **II** *ALPINE BOOTS*

8 Technology and Ski Boots

For decades, the ski boot maker's art did not change significantly until the 1960s, when Bob Lange introduced skiing's first plastic ski boot. Leather was replaced by high-tech plastics.

New technology made plastic a logical choice over leather for ski boots. Plastic was laterally rigid, held its shape, stood up to wear, and kept feet dry. Lange skied in his first prototype boot in 1957. But the new look in boots did not arrive until 1966 when Lange boots were worn by several racers in the 1966 World Championships. In 1968, Canada's Nancy Greene won her first World Cup title in the first season of World Cup racing while skiing in Lange boots.

The most significant step forward in ski boot design up until Lange's innovations was the introduction of the buckle. Henke, a popular choice of international racers, promoted its boots with the advertising slogan, "Are you still lacing while others are racing?" In 1968, most skiers on the World Cup circuit were wearing leather boots carefully stitched by Old World boot makers. But Lange's success sent boot makers scrambling to develop their own plastic boots. The leather boot was obsolete.

Lange first experimented with ABS plastic. Over the past twenty years, polyurethane has evolved as the most used plastic in ski boot shell manufacturing. Polyurethane is an elastomer (flexible, elastic type of material) that has a number of positive characteristics for use in ski boot shells. For example, it remains flexible through a wide range of temperatures. It will stiffen up to 40 percent between room temperature and −25 degrees Celsius or −13 degrees Farenheit. It has a low coefficient of friction, so it works well with ski bindings by providing consistent releases.

It has a hardness that is easily adapted to the structural needs of a ski boot. It molds thermally at a relatively low temperature. It has good abrasion-resistant characteristics to assure a reasonably long life under normal use.

Polyurethane accepts a wide range of colors, providing myriad cosmetic choices. Technically, it can be blended to adjust flex characteristics and thermal expansion and contraction characteristics of the boot. Given all of these qualities, polyurethane is the standard for most boots priced at the low to middle range.

More recently, polyethers have been used as boot shell material. Polyethers start with a polyurethane base that is altered, changing the molecular structure of the material. This altered structure has a lower density than polyurethane, providing a lighter-weight material.

Proponents of polyether claim that it has more consistent flex characteristics through a range of temperature variations. It is stiffer than polyurethane and has better mechanical strength than other materials.

Manufacturers who do not use polyether extensively admit that it has very good flex characteristics through a temperature range down to −15 degrees C or 5 degrees F. At that point, however, polyether becomes very firm and crystalline, and below that point, it becomes much stiffer than other materials.

In the past few years, nylons have been gaining in popularity among boot suppliers. Nylon has several interesting characteristics for ski boot fabrication. Many nylons have a specific density of 1.0 or less. Polyurethanes have a specific density of around 1.2. This lower density provides a significantly lighter-weight material.

Most nylons are stiffer than urethanes, and flex characteristics are altered by adding plasticizers. Nylon is less subject to temperature variations than polyurethanes. A polyamid (a type of nylon) has been developed which varies only 10 percent in temperature range, while polyurethane can vary up to 40 percent. Nylon has a lower coefficient of friction than polyurethane, providing a more consistent binding release.

Polyurethane is subject to degradation through exposure to ultraviolet (UV) radiation. Experienced skiers have observed that polyurethane boots discolor after exposure to the sun. Not only does the color of the boot fade but the plastic breaks down, becoming soft. Nylon is much more resistant to UV radiation. Some boots use nylon to provide rigidity and resiliency for rear and lateral support, while using spring devices or polyurethane components to allow forward flexibility.

On the negative side, nylon abrades. To combat this problem, nylon boots have wear pads on the boot soles made of a carbon rubber compound. These abrasion characteristics vary with different mixes. From a manufacturing point of view, nylon is difficult to mold: it requires a slightly higher temperature and is more difficult to release from a mold. Nylon also absorbs moisture, becoming softer and heavier with extensive use.

Nylons from the delrin and zytel families have been opening many new inroads in buckling devices and component attachments. Buckles and riveting devices of these materials are molded under extreme heat and very high pressures. These devices serve to lighten the weight of boots, provide more convenient closures, are warm to the touch in cold weather, are less expensive to assemble in manufacturing, and are more easily replaced in the field.

In the near future, we will probably see boots made of estane. Currently, this material is being used on the hubs of some front-wheel-drive cars. Estane offers consistent flexibility at all skiing temperatures. It is a very durable material but also very expensive.

All of the plastics currently used in boot manufacturing have given the skier longer-wearing boots. As boot makers learn more about the new materials available, boots will naturally offer better fit and performance.

9 *The Boot Shell*

Understanding the plastics that manufacturers use to build boot shells may satisfy the boot fitter's curiosity, but the search for the right boot actually begins with selecting the right size shell. Oversized boot shells are the most common cause of comfort, control, and support problems. Other fitting problems and cures will be covered below. Working from the outside in, unless you begin with the right size shell, boot modifications or fine tuning will be unnecessarily complicated, if not impossible.

The foot does need extra length in street shoes or running shoes because it actually becomes longer as it flexes. But footwear with rigid soles, which includes ski boots and ice skates, cannot be flexed, so the foot does not flex and does not need that extra room.

An orthotic or custom foot bed will often reduce the foot's tendency to elongate in length and to widen. That means that a shell that might have been too short without orthotics will be comfortable with orthotics without the need of additional modifications.

European sizes, the size marked on the inside of the shell, are one and a half sizes smaller than men's and two and a half sizes smaller than women's U.S. sizes. For example, a woman who wears a size 8 street shoe would wear a 5-1/2 ski boot made in Europe. A man with a size 7 foot would also take about a 5-1/2 European size. There is approximately one-third of an inch difference in shoe sizes in both U.S. and European sizes. Traditionally, manufacturers have made a new shell for every full size, or one-third of an inch, though there are exceptions. One shell size can be used to fit skiers with different shoe sizes by using different sized inner boots or insoles. The inner boot merely tries to make up for the differences between the shape of an individual skier's foot and the shape of a mass-produced last. A thicker insole takes up more volume and also adjusts length. For example, a size 4-1/2 shell with a thicker insole fits a size 4 foot.

It is also important not to confuse the sizes marked on the inside of the cuffs with boot sizes. Cuffs should not be used for sizing boots. They are usually marked with two sizes because one cuff size is used for every two shell sizes.

Shell shapes can also vary widely from one manufacturer to another and even between models produced by the same manufacturer. Although most boot manufacturers steer a middle course (building boots to fit the highest percentage of skiers), some skiers will discover the boot of choice may not provide the fit of choice.

A skier in the market for a new pair of boots could begin looking with a brand and model in mind but should be flexible enough to try other boots if the first choice does not offer the fit the skier is looking for.

Statistically, the average foot is a C width. Boot manufacturers try to accommodate this average. It is useful to check the shell size by trying on the boot without the liner. Pull the liner out and put the foot inside the shell to see how much space there is behind the heel. There should be about a half inch of space with the boot shell open. You can generally fit a skier with one-half to five-eighths of an inch, or three-eighths to one-half inch for racers. Once you realize how much space there is, you can see how much room there is for the liner to pack out. In a conventional boot, the toes can touch the front because the boot is designed to hold the foot down and back.

This shell test is not as valid for rear entry models as front entry boots because the liner configurations have more impact on the fit. You can put someone in a rear entry boot that is two sizes too big and still secure the foot by turning the levers and dials. When fitting a rear entry boot, make sure all the adjustments are in their wide open positions.

You can also use the boot board (the device under the liner which gives the foot its bottom support) as an aid in sizing rear entry boots. If the boot board spans the entire width and length of the boot shell, it can provide good information as to how well the foot matches the last of the boot shell. Remove the boot board from the boot shell and stand on it. With a sewn or lasted liner to compress, the foot should be about a sixth of an inch smaller than the perimeter of the boot board.

In front entry boots, like the four-buckle overlap shell, when the skier is standing straight up, the toes should just kiss the ends of the boots. In a flex-forward position, the toe should no longer be in contact. In most rear entry boots, as the skier puts the boot on, the toes should not touch at all. If they do, the touch should be barely perceptible. In a flexing motion, the foot should remain stable and should not slide back and forth along the floor of the boot. If you get a little slop, the chances are that the boot is a size or even a half size too big or adjustments need to be made with either the foot hold down or heel lift systems in the boot.

There are three basic questions you can ask to determine if the skier has the correct size. First, ask where the toes are. The skier should have the sensation of the toes touching the front of the inner boot. Second, ask if the skier can move his or her toes. Third, ask if the boot feels comfortable, if the foot feels snuggly held. If the answer is yes, we ask if there is any sensation of restriction of blood flow or any hot spots. If there are no unusual problems that require additional modifications, the chances are that the skier is in the right size boot.

Most boot fitters agree that it is not advisable to attempt to customize boots that are two or more shell sizes too large. But there are exceptions, for example, when the skier's feet are dramatically different in size. For skiers with a discrepancy of two or more sizes, for the smaller foot, use the firmest possible material to minimize compression and to maximize the transmission of energy. Normally, if there is about a size and a half difference, fit about half a size small on the large foot and fill for the smaller foot.

An important consideration in choosing the shell size is the shape of the foot relative to the size of the shell. Quite often, the inner boot is too short. That leaves too much space between the inner boot and the shell at the toe, or there is too much padding behind the heel which pushes the foot forward.

An important consideration is the shape of the toes and forefoot width relative to the width of the shell and the toe radius. The length may be right, but the toes can be crowded from the sides. In the late 1980s, there was a trend to more boxlike toes in ski boots. The fuller-volume fit is more in line with what was happening in the running shoe business. Early running shoe models were narrower than they are today. The idea then was to wrap the foot.

Today, the toe boxes are wider and fuller all the way around and provide more room for the foot to compress and contract. The foot needs extra room to expand because that extra width gained by impact helps distribute weight.

Most shops use the Brannock Device, the measuring instrument com-

monly used in shoe stores, to determine the initial boot size. A special Brannock for ski boots measures about half a size smaller than the standard Brannock. This device provides a ball of the foot to heel measurement, determines the location of the widest part of the foot, and indicates a letter designation for width. It also determines the length of the foot as it relates to the arch length.

The ideal Brannock measurement is to come up with the same number designation for both heel to ball of foot measurement and for foot length measurement. Most skiers either fall into the average category or have short toe measurements. Skiers in the latter category can still obtain a perfect fit, but there will be extra room in the toe area.

For skiers with a longer than average toe measurement, finding and fitting the right shell can be more complicated. With long toes, the ball of the foot to heel length will be shorter than the toe to heel measurement. To provide enough length for the toes, the ball of the foot ends up being behind the widest part of the boot and the arch behind the arch support. To receive an ideal fit in this case, the shell will need to be reshaped with a stretcher and the boot board and insole recontoured with a grinding tool. Use a toe to heel measurement.

An exception to the Brannock Device measuring system is the Salomon's boot fitting system, which chooses shell sizes by measuring the skier's foot based on the loop from the heel around over the instep, which essentially measures foot volume. In all cases, whether using the Brannock Device or Salomon's system, the measurements provide the information you need to make an initial boot shell selection. They provide a beginning point.

The final choice will be influenced by whether the liner is hand lasted or molded. A lasted liner will stretch because it is more like a shoe. After a few days of wear, the liner tends to accommodate the shape of the foot. With continual use, it will compress and may require the use of fitting materials. Molded liners do not stretch as much, so the fit you get when trying on a boot is close to the fit that will remain. The interior wicking sock used in injected liners compresses somewhat but not to the same extent as materials used in a lasted or sewn liner.

Molded technology mirrors the inside of the shell. The material used today is very dense, and the technology for making molded inner boots has improved dramatically in the past few years. At one time, there was a separation problem where the snow cuff was attached to the molded liner. That has largely been overcome. Molded liners were used originally in less expensive boots, but the improvements in technology have encouraged their use in good-quality boots.

Competitors and skiers looking for maximum performance tend to choose the smallest possible boot shell. The less padding used between the foot and the shell, the more responsive the system will be. The reason for the liner is to cushion the skin against a rigid shell, to provide insulation, and to wick moisture from the foot. The compromise is in how to do it in a quarter of an inch or less.

Keeping padding to a minimum is like driving a sports car. The more rigid the steering, the more precise the control. It is the same thing between the foot and the boot. The more rigid the linkage, the more precisely things will happen.

The loss is also similar to a sports car. If you sit in a sports car for a hundred miles, you know you have driven a hundred miles. It is a rougher ride. If you drive in a Chevrolet, however, a hundred miles is no problem. But you do not have the compassion for the road that you do in a sports car. In boots, softer is easier, but you lose some precision.

It is important to remember that the body has to absorb all that jarring and shock. That is the penalty. Some racers are macho to the point of being masochistic. Research seems to indicate that the body will not ignore pain. Boots that hurt your feet can distract from concentration and performance. A good fit is important for performance, but a boot that is too small can be self-defeating.

10 Fitting Rear Entry Boots

Today's ski boots have evolved from yesterday's hiking boots. And today's ski boot fitting systems began with leather boots that laced up the front. As boot materials changed from leather to plastic, synthetic materials offered boot makers new design options. One was the rear entry boot, which entered the market in 1970. These boots now account for the majority of boot sales worldwide.

As you look at the boots introduced in the last few years, rear entry boots look more like front entry systems. At the same time, front entry boots are incorporating more and more of the designs that were created by the rear entry revolution. Some newer boot models are basically rear entry boots with front overlap buckle systems.

Although front entry systems and rear entry boots are growing closer in concept, there are still differences in fit adjustments and corrections. Some fit problems are more common with one type of system than the other. And there are fitting tricks that make it easier to work with a specific type of boot.

Whether the boot is front or rear entry, each brand of boot, and often varying models within a brand, will offer a different shape. The best fit is achieved when the skier finds a boot that has a shape consistent with his foot. Lasted and sewn boot liners compress with use, making the fit looser. Make sure the initial fit allows for these changes.

Knowing the System

In rear entry boots, a greater amount of force from the closure system is applied to the back and sides of the leg and around the heel. In a front closure system, there is often more compression of the forefoot and front of the leg due to the buckles.

Front entry boots seem to create problems with arch cramping because of the stretching of the arch area when the boot is closed from above. Rear entry boots develop more instep pressure points caused by cable systems that create a line of pressure. These pressures are often compounded in

rear entry boots by a very defined instep shape that does not change or conform with buckle adjustments.

Although sweeping generalizations are risky when discussing boot fit, in rear entry boots, more fit problems need to be addressed with liner alterations, whereas shell mismatches are a greater cause of fit problems with front entry systems. When you close the buckles on a front entry boot, the entire architectural structure of the shell is drawn in against the foot. If the shape of that shell varies from the foot it encompasses, discomfort is going to result at the points of nonconformity.

With a typical rear closure, the mechanisms for securing the foot are not as rigid as the boot shell. These mechanisms do, however, exert a tremendous amount of force on the liner. Hard components in the liner (and mismatches between the compressed liner's shape and the foot) will soon become points of aggravation. It is amazing how hard a piece of sponge can become when all the air is forced from it.

With a front entry boot, a fitter will spend more time using heat and a stretching device to mold the boot shell to the shape of the skier's foot. With a rear closure boot, the fitter spends more time with a die grinder, razor, glue, and pads to eliminate nonconformities from the liner.

Solving Rear Entry Problems

Working with rear entry boots is often more difficult than with front entry systems. The liners are often harder to remove from the boot shell. A heel tab on the back of the boot liner fits under the rear spoiler pad on a number of rear entry boots.

To remove the liner from the shell, the heel tab first must be pulled from under the back pad. Usually, simple finger strength is all that is needed to fold the back pad out of the way and free the heel tab. When reinserting the boot liner, the heel tab must again be installed under the back pad. This operation often involves digital isometrics. Several rear entry boots incorporate tabs that lock the liner to the boot shell. These shell tabs have a catch that has to be compressed for the liner to slide off the tab. When reinstalling the liner, the tab is reinserted.

Before attempting to remove the liner from a rear entry boot, any forefoot and heel-instep tension adjustments (buckling systems) must be loosened.

Internal Hardware

With several boot models, care must be taken not to catch internal hardware (especially the pressure plate) on the boot's shin cuff and instep adjustment cable. If the liner resists being pulled from the boot, slip it back into place and investigate at the instep and heel for any internal parts that might be catching.

Sometimes, liners in rear entry boots fit into the shell so tightly that it is difficult for mortal man to remove the liner from the shell manually. In this case, either find an immortal to remove the liner or grip the heel of the liner with a vise grip or channel lock and pull. A word of caution: be sure components are not hung up on one another before tugging with a tool. Be gentle. It is possible to tear the liner material.

The number one fit problem in popular rear entry boots is upper instep pressure. With any boot, however, there are technological limitations that result in common fit problems. If you understand the cause of those problems and know some possible solutions, the fit of the boots can be improved.

Looking at the liner at the point of discomfort, note the seam within the liner's interior. The Salomon-type liners are constructed with a foam-backed cloth covering the shin and ankle area which is separate from the piece of material that encompasses the foot. The seam that joins these two pieces of material is bulky. It is at the point where the heel/instep retention cable fits over the pressure plate. The heel/instep cable exerts tremendous force at that point.

Adjustable Front Cuff

Some rear entry models with an adjustable front cuff (forward lean adjustment) have screws that anchor the cuff from the medial and lateral sides of the boot's upper shaft. When the skier flexes forward against the boot cuff, it pivots at those screws.

The lower edge of the cuff rocks back against the upper instep very close to where the seam is in the liner. The tendon of the tibialis anterior muscle often protrudes from the skier's instep. When the cable, pressure plate, and liner seam are pressed against a dominant instep and a protruding tendon, pain results.

The first step in dealing with this problem is to lock the front cuff so it cannot pivot. This is done by drilling a small hole through the boot's shaft and the lower edge of the front cuff, then installing a rivet or "T-nut" in the hole. Next, pad the liner with strips of dense 1/8-inch material above and below the point where the seam lies in the liner. The purpose of the pads is to bridge the pressure plate and heel/instep cable so it does not apply pressure to the seam.

If the boot has an injected (urethane foam) liner, reduce the exterior surface of the liner directly over the seam with a hand-grinding tool, so it can give at that point. Usually, these steps solve the problem. If more work is needed, undo the seam with a seam ripper or a razor. Straighten the material layers with the upper material overlapping the lower. Glue the materials together with a thin, smooth bead of Aquaseal.

Back-of-the-Heel Discomfort

Discomfort at the back of the heel is common with rear entry boots. Several components of the boot meet at the top side of the heel, pressing against one another and creating frequent pressure points. With most rear entry boots, when the rear spoiler is closed, the back pad closes over a heel tab, which closes over the back edge of the boot liner.

The boot liner usually has "L" pads installed or molded into the back of the liner to provide heel retention. Of course, the heel tab and back pad close over these "L" pads. If the skier has a bony heel, he will be prone to discomfort in that area. If the boot has been down-sized for performance reasons, the problems will be more pronounced.

The first step is to locate exactly where the boot components are causing the aggravation. With the skier wearing a pair of socks, coat the outside of the sock with soft chalk at the point of discomfort. Have the skier put the boot on and flex. The chalk will leave an impression at the problem area.

Remove the boot from the skier's foot and close the boot's buckles. Shine a flashlight into the boot so you can see the chalk marks. Note all the materials that overlap that point and mark their location. Kwik Ski Products and Technology and Tools both sell rear entry push pads. Occasionally, the problem can be dealt with quickly and cheaply by placing a pair of these pads behind the back pad just above the point of discomfort.

Overlapping Materials

Sometimes it is necessary to cut away the overlapping materials one layer at a time until you create a deep enough channel to eliminate the problem. Start with the heel tab; remove a portion or all of it. If the problem still persists, reduce material from the boot liner at the pressure point. The last component usually is the back pad. This progression may vary with the boot. When evaluating the problem area, always look objectively at the components. With a good eye, you can pick out the part causing the trouble.

It is a fact of life that most ski boots are purchased too large. A majority of boot manufacturers fabricate their boots on the wide side. It is easier to sell a boot that is too roomy than one that is too snug. Given the adjustment capability of rear entry boots, it is possible to secure a foot in a boot that is significantly too large. This can eliminate tactile awareness, sacrificing performance and creating pressure points from the closure mechanisms.

Reducing excess volume is a prime concern in refitting rear entry boots. There are a number of fit aids that have been created for use with rear entry boots. Many of the fit aids created originally for front entry systems are also well suited for rear entry boots.

Flo Fit Technology

The Flo Fit Corporation in Boulder, Colorado, has created some fit aids that are quite effective. They evolved from rear entry technology. To secure the forefoot and midfoot, they offer the Snugs Instep Pad. If only the heel area is loose, Snugs Ankle Pads fit over the heel and instep region. For securing the entire foot, Flo Fit supplies Pro Performance Pacs that fill in around most of the foot.

A more specific, custom fit is attained with the Snugs Racing Performance Pac, which is a flow injection system. It not only reduces volume but also molds to the shape of the foot and the boot shell. It smooths pressures against the foot and creates intimate contact between the liner and shell, improving tactile awareness and performance.

Foam fit aids are available in several configurations to reduce volume in rear entry boots. Saddle pads fit over the instep and around the ankles. They provide a tighter-fitting heel cup as well as relieve pressure from the ankles in a rear entry boot. Saddle/Side pads are elongated versions of the saddle pad. They not only secure the rear of the foot, but secure the sides of the forefoot as well.

Rear entry instep pads secure the heel for an individual with a low instep region and perhaps a wider heel. Foam fit aids can be trimmed with a pair of scissors or razor to accommodate misshapen areas or to avoid overlapping hardware in the boot.

Narrowing Pads

Although not designed specifically for rear entry boots, narrowing pads (or side pads) work very well in reducing the volume of a rear entry boot. They have the advantage of not going over the instep. Occasionally, saddle pads can create pressure in this area. It is not desirable in many instances to apply pressure where a seam might exist.

Several rear entry boots have hardware in the back of the boot which causes lateral or outside ankle pressure point problems. The fit of a rear entry boot is obtained from a cable that wraps the heel instep region. In several cases, that cable attaches to the lateral side of the boot's shaft. People with small feet and dominant outside ankle bones often develop discomfort from the ankle striking the attachment of that cable. The cable attaches with a rivet on the interior of the boot shell. The solution is to drill out the rivet that anchors the cable and rivet the cable to the exterior of the boot shell.

Velcro Strap

Some boot models have a Velcro strap above the heel. The strap attaches to the interior of the boot shell with metal "D" rings. A skier with large outside ankle bones will feel pressure against these rings. The purpose of the Velcro strap is tightening or loosening the heel cup. The solution to the ankle problem is to remove the entire assembly (drilling out the rivets that hold it in place) and install rear entry push pads or felt tongue pads to tighten the heel cup.

If an individual has a problem foot, or wants the tailored fit and performance of a foam-injected boot, Sidas manufactures a replacement foam liner for rear entry boots. The cost is high, but the fit is great. Many World Cup racers who use rear entry boots have the Sidas foam liner. One manufacturer is in the process of developing a foam inner boot.

Custom Footbeds

For the most part, there is no difference between installing a custom footbed (orthotic) in a rear entry boot and in a front entry boot. It is mandatory that the custom footbed be the same length as the stock insole found in the rear entry boot. Rear entry boots usually have long toe boxes. If the footbed is trimmed or cast to the foot's length, it will be too short for the boot. The short footbed will have a tendency to creep forward. If you are using footbed blanks that have a tendency to shrink in the heating process, as most do, be certain to start with an extra-long footbed blank (core). When installing the footbed in a boot that has an injected liner, any posting material used on the bottom of the footbed must be beveled excessively to fit around the arch contour molded in the liner.

Over the past few years, rear entry boots have made up the majority of boots being sold at retail. Now, fitting rear entry boots is not the exception but the norm. The key element in fitting rear entry boots is using logic and looking objectively at each fit. Every situation is different. That is what makes boot fitting a perpetually creative challenge.

Boot suppliers provide fitting information in their service manuals and some basic fitting data in material included in the box with the boots. Since shop technicians are often asked to work with boots the shop does not sell, the general information included here should prove useful.

11 *Built-in Boot Adjustments*

Once the correct size boot is selected, most fit modifications and fine tuning can be completed with built-in fitting devices. Forward lean, forward flex, shaft cant, heel lift, arch support, and wedging are features incorporated into boots to make them fit the individual skier. These adjustments can dramatically improve a skier's balance, finesse, performance, and comfort.

Adjustments come in many forms. Some are as easy as turning a dial. At the other extreme are adjustment devices that require special tools. Not all of the possible boot adjustments are obvious. In addition, changes in some boot adjustments can affect other characteristics. The state of the art in ski boots is realized only when each adjustment is modified to suit the individual.

The adjustment options built into each manufacturer's boots vary from model to model and from year to year. While it is impossible to discuss all the adjustments available on all boot models, the types of adjustment devices tend to fall into identifiable categories.

As an additional aid to fitting, boot suppliers include detailed adjustment instructions in the boot box.

Forward Lean

Forward lean, which balances a skier's center of mass, is the most common performance adjustment on ski boots. Too much forward lean causes the skier to stand in a low position, overusing the muscles of the thighs and hips. Too little reduces the skier's ability to edge the ski and perform short radius turns. Finding the proper position usually involves hill testing until the optimal levels of quickness, comfort, and balance are attained.

Forward lean affects balance, quickness, range of motion, muscular strain, knee strain, and nerve circulation. It is related to the forward pitch of the boot's shaft or collar. More forward lean creates more bend in the knee and hip. For the knee joint to articulate medially and laterally (inside and outside), the knee must first be flexed or bent. The deeper the knee is bent, the more the camlike knee opens. Thus, the more the knee is

bent, the farther it can be driven toward the medial side. Greater forward lean allows a more dramatic roll of the ski onto its edge.

People looking for an aggressive checking motion prefer more forward lean, as when skiing steep, narrow chutes or short, ledgey moguls. Skiers looking for a subtler contact with the edge prefer a more upright stance.

The tremendous torsional rigidity of current racing skis provides a smoother turning radius with subtler edging moves. Torsionally softer cruiser-type skis come alive with more forward lean and more aggressive edging motions.

More forward lean requires greater strength in the quadricep muscles, the major muscles in front of the thigh. A person who is not in prime physical condition should have a more upright stance.

Increased forward lean lowers a person's center of gravity, improving

static balance. Tall people often ski better with greater forward lean. Skiing is dynamic, however. Increasing forward lean reduces the range of motion available in the joints. With ideal biomechanics, an individual will have 20 degrees of forward motion available in the ankle. This range of motion aids in balance recovery, so too much forward lean hinders recovery from an unbalanced moment. This problem is more evident with shorter people than with taller individuals, because of their lack of leverage.

Many people have far less than 20 degrees of forward flex available in their ankles. A tight Achilles tendon often leads to a lack of mobility in the ankle. Excessive forward lean for an individual with poor ankle mobility will lever the forefoot into the bottom of the boot. This leads to numbness in the toes and forefoot as well as cramping or muscle strain in the arch. Changing the forward lean will alter pressure on the shin and instep, possibly solving shin bite problems. Increasing forward lean will move pressure upward.

Forward lean adjusters come in many forms. Wedged spoilers are used by a number of companies to vary forward lean. A forward lean spoiler will increase the angle of the shaft approximately four degrees. Several manufacturers have incorporated forward lean shims into their designs. These shims have a secondary function of removing volume from the shaft of the boot. A person with thin legs, or long lower legs, will appreciate the thinning effect of a forward lean shim.

The most common form of forward lean adjustment is a finger nut on a threaded rod located on the back of a

front entry boot. Turn the nut one direction and it moves up the rod, driving the upper shaft of the boot forward. This adjustment is usually on
the same hardware module that adjusts forward flex. Often, increasing
the forward lean will stiffen the forward flex as well and reduce the range
of flex.

Some rear entry boots use a repo-
sitionable front tab to alter forward
lean. The front tab attaches to the
front of the boot shell with a screw on
the inside and outside edge. When the
screws are removed, the tab can be
repositioned forward to increase forward lean or rearward to decrease it.
When the tab is moved forward, there
is an enlargement in shaft volume.
When the Salomon front is moved
rearward, or forward lean is de-
creased, shaft volume is reduced.
Forward lean adjustments are usually
accompanied by adjustments in the fit
cable on the shaft to compensate for
volume changes.

Another common adjustment involves a ratchet adjustment on the
back of the boot to alter forward lean.
A second adjustment alters the collar
at the top of the boot. The collar can
be driven forward to increase forward
lean or drawn back to decrease it.

Plastic wedges are another option
some boot makers use. These
wedges can be pressed between the
upper shaft and the lower shell to
drive the shaft forward and increase
forward lean. The wedges come in
several thicknesses to provide differing degrees of lean, and they will work
with a number of front entry boots
that do not have forward lean
adjusters.

Other devices being built into current models include a wing assembly

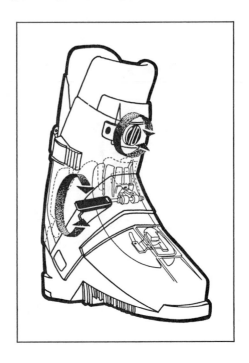

on the back of the upper cuff which
hinges away from the back of the boot
and is rotated to drive the boot shaft
forward or backward. Another device
is an asymmetric block between the
inner shell and the shaft. The upper
cuff of the boot is disengaged by removing the cant adjustment screw at
the lateral side of the cuff. The cuff
can then be pulled away from the shell
and the forward lean block repositioned. Two blocks, which anchor on a tab
on the lower shell, come with each
boot. By turning the asymmetric
blocks upside down, the blocks can
establish four differing forward lean
positions.

A forward lean adjuster in the front
cuff is an easy-to-use finger adjuster.
Turn the screw one way and the front
cuff is pulled forward over the lower
shell. Turn it the other way and the
shaft is straightened.

One rear closure boot has an adjustment to control forward lean from the
back of the boot. A post on the boot's

rear spoiler has a screw adjustment. Turning this device drives the back spoiler farther forward when the rear buckle is closed.

Forward Flex

Forward flex has to do with the amount of resistance or leverage a boot transmits to a ski from ankle flexion. Softer flex implies that a boot is absorbing a major portion of ankle flexion. If ankle flexion is absorbed by the boot, then it is not transferred to the ski where that motion would force the shovel into reverse camber or into a turn. Softer flex in a boot reduces ski reactions and is a forgiving characteristic.

Stiffer flex implies that forward bend in the ankle becomes a levering force from the leg, through the boot, to the ski. The ski forebody will react by arcing. If the ski is on edge, it will turn. So a stiffer boot correlates to a more energetic, quicker response from the ski.

The ankle joint is capable of supple forward motions. When a ski accelerates, ankle flexion moves a skier's center of mass forward, helping to maintain balance. When the tip of the ski encounters obstacles, flexion at the ankle absorbs much of the resulting shock, maintaining balance. Softer flex enhances balance in these two instances by allowing freer ankle motion.

If a ski rapidly decelerates, the skier uses the top of the boot as a brace to resist toppling forward. A stiffer boot will provide better bracing for maintaining balance in this situation.

A tall, heavy, or strong person has more leverage or mass to work forward flexion in a ski boot. A larger per-

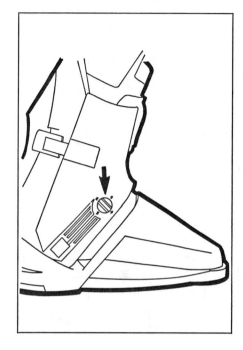

son requires sturdier resistance during deceleration, requiring a stiffer flex. Conversely, a short or light person will not have the leverage or mass to work the boot. This person needs a softer flex.

When boots are too stiff for a skier, they will lock the ankles. To compensate for this lack of flexion at the ankle, the individual will bend excessively at the knee and hip. The result is a squatting or sitting back position. A boot with too much forward lean in the shaft further aggravates this position. Softening the flex of the boot and reducing the forward lean in the cuff will dramatically improve this person's skiing ability.

Flex adjustments work in one of two ways. The most effective involves increasing the grip between the upper cuff of a boot and the lower shell. A major number of front entry systems and some rear entry boots use compression springs to control flex. The upper cuff of the boot articu-

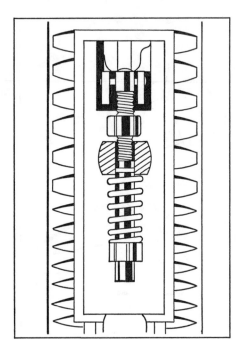

lates against a spring, which is anchored to the lower boot shell. To stiffen the flex of these systems, a nut tightens over the spring and compresses it. The more tightly the spring is compressed, the less motion is allowed in the upper cuff.

Several boots use a cam, which, when turned one way, blocks motion of the cuff against the shell. Turned the other, it allows free travel over several millimeters. Incremental gradations of motion are allowed between the two extremes.

A second type of flex adjustment system involves changing the leverage point at the top of the boot. Raising the height of the front cuff increases the skier's leverage and the ability to apply power through the front of the boot. Decreasing the height of the front cuff reduces the skier's mechanical advantage over the boot shell. A variation of this adjustment opens or closes the front cuff of the boot to raise or lower the leverage point on the boot.

Canting

Canting involves tipping the upper part of the boot to match the angle of a person's lower leg, thereby balancing the lower leg so the knee is perpendicular to the ski's bottom surface.

A person who needs canting adjustment has difficulty riding a flat ski without it. If he is bowlegged, he catches outside edges and crosses the tails of his skis. A person who is knock-kneed catches inside edges and crosses his ski tips. Skiers who need cant adjustment feel as if they are slow gliders, always being passed in the schusses.

As all good boot fitters know, canting is ineffective if the foot is excessively pronated. So before much energy is spent on cant adjustment, the bottom of the foot needs to be fitted. Once the foot is properly fitted, canting can make a significant difference in an individual's skiing ability.

An outwardly bowed lower leg tips the boot sole and the ski onto its outside edge. To compensate for bowed legs, an individual will drive his knees inward to achieve a flat ski. So a bowlegged individual will ski knock-kneed. The shaft of the ski boot should be tipped out until the individual's knee is over the second ball of _TOE_ the foot when the boot sole is flat.

The most common shaft cant involves a screw clamp on one side of the boot shaft. The clamp is disconnected and the boot shaft is manually tipped until the proper alignment is achieved. Then the side of the cuff is reclamped.

Some boots have systems with a threaded shaft on the side of the boot. Turning a screw head on that shaft moves the outside edge of the shaft up or down to realign the shaft relative to the boot sole.

Cam systems are also widely used. The cam is located under a cover on the side of the boot shaft. Sole canting allows compensation for the lower leg angle by changing the foundation on which the boot rests. As with a shaft cant, the wedged boot soles are changed until the center of the knee mass aligns over the second toe.

Heel Lift

Forward lean in the boot shaft is closely aligned to lift in the heel. An individual who has a tight Achilles tendon will have difficulty flexing forward in the ankle. People who wear high-heeled shoes or who do not accompany lower body athletics with adequate stretching exercises will acquire these problems. Some people genetically have tight muscle and tendon structures. Traumatic damage to the bones or fibrous material in the lower leg and foot can also reduce ankle mobility.

The result is difficulty in flexing a ski boot and discomfort when a boot forces the ankle into a flexed position. Since no flexion is available in the ankle, a person with these problems is prone to sitting back when skiing, even when the forward flex of the boot is quite soft.

When the heel is raised in the ski boot, tension is removed from the back of the leg and Achilles tendon. The ankle is repositioned into a stance where it has a range of mobility. The

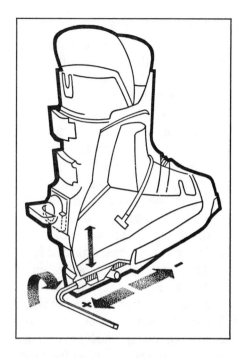

skier can bring his hips forward if the ankle can flex.

The boot board is the plastic or foam foundation found below the liner in a ski boot. Heel lift adjustments use a wedge in the heel area of the board. When a threaded shaft is turned, a part is forced to travel along with the wedge, forcing the heel area of the boot upward.

Raising the heel also drives the instep into the top of the boot, snugging the instep-heel region. In addition, raising the heel changes the shape of the heel cup, altering pressures on the heel.

Arch Adjusters

A high-arched individual often has a focus of pressure on the balls of the feet (metatarsal heads), which can cause discomfort, burning, and numbing sensations. The arch becomes fatigued when it is not supported.

Some boots are built with an adjustable arch—a wedge on a threaded shaft. When the shaft is turned, the wedge is pressed under an arch support. The arch support, in turn, lifts. That support can fill the void in the bottom of a high-arched foot and greatly enhance comfort.

The major cause of foot discomfort in ski boots is excessive pronation, which involves foot instabilities that significantly hinder performance. The varus wedge is the basic fit aid used to improve a common pronated foot.

The great attribute of built-in adjustments is that they give the skier and the boot fitter a means of tinkering and testing. Boot fitting is a process that often involves trial and error. With built-ins, you can test different characteristics without permanently altering a boot. It helps to have some technical knowledge for the basis of these adjustments before making changes. Misadjusting these built-ins can ruin a day's skiing. Once these adjustments are dialed in correctly, skiing gets easier, more comfortable, and more fun.

12 *Fit Aids*

F it aids are to a boot fitter what a chisel is to a sculptor. They are the basic tools of the trade. The logical progression in boot fitting is to first use the built-in adjustments on the boot (see preceding section) before using fit aids. Finally, you can change the configuration of the boot through sanding, grinding, or shell expansion.

Several fitting functions can be performed with the use of fit aids: (1) you can fill excess volume, and (2) the position or stability of the foot can be altered and pressure can be redistributed to relieve high points and fill voids. In most cases, the best fit aids are made of dense, noncompressible materials. The objective in adding fit aids is first to secure the foot. Compressible fit materials yield to the strong forces applied to a boot when skiing. The result is ineffectiveness in attempting to secure or stabilize the foot. Therefore, good materials for boot fitting include high density foams, rubber, felt, and flow.

Working under the Foot

Good boot fitters usually start from the bottom of the foot and work up. The philosophy is that you should begin with a good foundation and then worry about constructing the walls. Of course, the best fit aids for the bottom of the foot are a pair of well-constructed footbeds—orthotic devices (see below).

There are a number of under-foot fit aids that are "off-the-shelf" items. They will perform some of the functions of a custom footbed. The most common is the insole. Most current upper-end ski boots are being made with a reasonable "anatomic insole."

A good insole provides cupping to help stabilize the heel. The insole should be of a relatively firm and highly insulative material. Far more heat can be lost through the bottom of the foot through conduction than through the sides and the top of the boot. The top surface of a good insole has cushioning and moisture wicking

59

capabilities. A good insole also provides support under the arch.

Shims, which are often referred to as insoles, are fillers that can go either under the boot's liner or inside the liner under the anatomic insole to reduce the volume of the boot. Shims are made of polyethylene, Bontex (a water-resistant cardboard), or polyethyl foam. Shims differ from insoles in not having a distinguishable heel cup, arch support, or cushioning top surface.

Think of boots as a pyramid. When the underside of the foot is filled, the foot is usually moved into a smaller part of the boot. Shims are most effective with a pancake-shaped foot. When a foot is thin, with a high instep, filling under the foot with a shim will often create aggravation at the instep and numbness under the forefoot without effectively stopping the side-to-side motion of the heel.

The varus wedge is the basic device to ease the symptoms of the simple pronated foot. Symptoms of the pronated foot include inside ankle pain, arch fatigue, toe bang, discomfort of the little toe, bunions at the inside ball of the foot, and shin bite.

The varus wedge creates an inclined plane under the heel. Raising the inside of the heel lifts the arch, draws the toes back, twists the forefoot inward, and rotates the lower leg outward. It improves the stability and power of the foot.

An arch support (navicular pad or long pad) fills the arch cavity. When used in conjunction with a varus wedge, it will help reduce the symptoms of a pronated foot. The arch support reduces pressure at the forefoot, easing the tension that causes numbing under the toes and the ball of the foot.

The heel lift has been referred to as the aspirin of boot fitting. If you do not know what else to do, add a heel lift. It may help. A heel lift raises the ankle bones, changing their relationship with the ankle cups. It will change the pressure distribution over the instep and the lower shin.

Raising the heel pivots the foot at the instep, drawing the toes away from the front of the boot. Lifting the heel elevates the calf in relation to the boot's collar—often reducing calf discomfort and pinching. It also reduces the direct pressure at the arch.

A heel lift reduces flexion at the ankle, easing tension in the calf and pressure under the forefoot. Usually glued under an anatomic insole, it will alter a skier's stance and balance.

A heel cup performs the functions of the heel lift with the additional benefit of cradling under the heel bone. It is usually made of a cushioning type of material that can relieve the discomfort of a heel spur or a skin disorder under the heel bone. The heel cup is usually glued to the top of an insole so it is directly against the foot.

A metatarsal pad acts as a bridge, spreading pressure from the inner and outer balls of the foot across the forward portion of the foot and is usually glued to the bottom of a flexible insole. When properly positioned, a metatarsal pad can relieve numbing under the first two toes or the outside toes.

Wedged insoles tip the entire plane the foot rests on. There are some pronated feet that do not respond to a varus wedge under the heel, and in this case, the foot often shows an inward tip in the forefoot.

When the skier's weight is applied to the forefoot, the weight forces the inner edge of the forefoot to the floor.

The result is a collapsing of the arch, creating the fit problems associated with pronation. A wedged insole under the liner, or under the anatomic insole in the liner, will support the forefoot in its inwardly tipped posture, reducing the problems associated with pronation.

Encompassing the Foot

After supporting and stabilizing the bottom of the foot, the sides, top, and heel area can be properly fitted. Fit aids can be trimmed and matched to fill the voids that exist between the foot and the liner. They can be bonded to the outside of the liner to remove pressure from the high spots and to apply pressure to the low spots.

The narrowing pad fits on the side of the boot liner and reduces the volume of the liner significantly. The narrowing pad comes in two different configurations, the standard or modified narrowing pad.

The standard narrowing pad (often referred to as a side pad) wraps over the ankle and side of the foot. The modified narrowing pad is cut out to provide a channel for the ankle. It fills the side of the foot and fills in front of and below the ankle. Most narrowing pads have a self-adhesive backing produced by 3M.

Pads are always applied to the outer surface of the liner. Sometimes silicone is used to aid in sliding a liner into the boot shell. So, before applying a narrowing pad, you may need to clean the outside surface of the liner. A mild solvent applied to the liner will lift any contaminants. Remove the solvent with a paper towel.

To assure that the pad adheres well to the liner, apply a good adhesive such as a Master cement or a Barge cement. Let the glue dry until it is tacky. Remove the paper backing from the pad and apply it to the liner. If the skier's foot has notable bumps or high points on the side of the foot, it may be necessary to cut areas out of the narowing pad where the high points exist. It may be advisable to trim the front end of a narrowing pad down so that it does not overlap the ball of the foot. Beveling the edges of many thick pads with a sander improves the transition to the pad.

The wraparound pad encompasses the back of the liner of a front entry boot. It reduces heel lift dramatically and will stop side-to-side slop in the heel. If properly positioned, a wraparound can spread the pressure from a bunion at the back of the heel.

Wraparound pads come in two configurations—standard and modified. The standard wraparound incorporates "C"-type configurations to surround the ankle bones. The modified wraparound fits above the heel with wings that fill below the ankle bones. Wraparound pads have been designed for use exclusively in front entry systems.

Saddle pads reduce the rear foot volume in a rear entry boot. They fit over the instep and around the sides of the heel on a rear entry boot liner. A full saddle pad, unlike a rear foot saddle pad, narrows the sides of the liner in addition to filling the rear foot region.

"C" pads can surround an ankle bone or a bunion, spreading pressure from that point. In their most common usage, the "C" pads fit above, behind, and below the ankle. Not only will they relieve pressure from the points they surround but they will also significantly tighten the heel area. In many rear entry configurations, the "C" pad is placed backward, above, in front of and below the ankle to avoid complications with the tab and rear liner behind, and above the heel.

"L" pads are intended to thin the boot liner on the sides of the Achilles tendon and below the heel. Like "C" pads, they will relieve some pressure from the ankle.

Snugs Flopacs do a great job of filling various areas of a boot while at the same time molding to the shape of the foot, relieving pressure from the high points. Snugs come in a number of varying shapes and configurations. Probably the most useful is the performance pad. This pad wraps around the heel and sides of the boot liner. The Flo is a malleable material that moves from the high points and fills in the voids.

The Snugs Injection Flopac is effective in eliminating large areas of excess volume. It is bonded to the inside of the boot shell, then the boot liner is inserted under it and the Flo is pumped into the pack until the boot is snugged.

If, after use, the pack proves to be overfilled, you simply pull the plug, flex the boot, and Flo material will be driven from the pack. These Injection Flopacs come in both front entry and rear entry configurations.

Cuff Padding

The shaft area of the boot is one of the most critical areas to fit. No activity other than skiing puts stress on that particular region of the body.

Felt tongue pads are versatile fit aids that are good at effecting small changes in the cuff area. Shin bite is often caused by a sharp, dominant tibia in the individual's lower leg. When the individual flexes into a boot, that dominant bone strikes the shell before pressure is applied to the fleshy sides of the leg. Tongue pads can be used to fill the liner to the sides of the tibia, spreading pressure away from that bone.

If a skier has a very thin leg, there will be lots of excess motion in the top of the boot. When the leg reaches the end of the gap, it slams against the boot, and discomfort results. The tapered shin pad fits on the front of the boot tongue or down the front of a rear entry boot to reduce extra space and to cushion the shin.

The collar wrap is placed on the back of the liner at the calf or is bonded to the boot shell to reduce volume at the top of the boot. In a rear entry boot, a collar wrap can be placed around the front side of the liner. In a rear entry boot, the arms of the collar

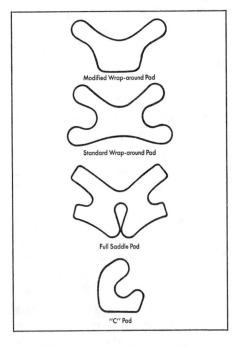

Modified Wrap-around Pad

Standard Wrap-around Pad

Full Saddle Pad

"C" Pad

wrap often require trimming so they are not peeled back by the overlapping components of the boot collar.

Good fit aids offer quick, effective alterations in the fit of a ski boot. They also offer the advantage, in most cases, of being reversible alterations.

13 *Boot Liners*

A ski boot's liner is responsible for many of the key characteristics of a good boot. The liner provides cushioning for critical areas. It should contour into the low areas of the foot, providing security and control. It also provides most of a boot's insulation. It should wick perspiration away from the skier's foot for warmth, and, ideally, should dry quickly. It should be firm enough to provide good transmission of foot steering through the outer shell and to the ski. It should have enough integrity that it does not break down, causing degeneration of the boot's fit. Yet, the liner should be adaptable enough that a boot fitter can sculpt it to significantly different foot shapes.

Boot manufacturers use three types of liners. Each has its strengths and weaknesses.

Sewn Liners

In many lower- to mid-priced boots, sewn liners are employed. In these liners, materials are drawn off rolls and are die cut to specific shapes. These materials are then sewn and glued into a pattern intended to match a foot's shape. The interior material of the liner is generally a nylon or wool material. It is often backed by a thin layer of pliable foam. Wherever there is a low spot (e.g., around the ankles and above the heel), thick layers of foam are laminated into place to match the low areas. In places where liners need rigidity, sheets of stiffening materials in the form of fiberboard or plastic are inserted. The exterior of the liner is usually a vinyl or sometimes a nylon material.

Sewn liners generally utilize fairly soft foams and other materials that are intended to compress to the shape of an individual's foot. Since these materials are compressible, the interior of the liner tends to expand and become significantly larger with use. When a skier buys a boot with a sewn liner, it should be very tight, perhaps a bit too small. After the boot is worn for a period of time, the liner will grow to the shape of the foot. With a sewn boot liner, the approach used to fit a new boot should involve shell size or boot board sizing.

Lasted Liners

Lasted liners are similar to sewn boot liners in many ways. Sheets of materials are die cut to specific patterns, then stitched or laminated together. The major difference is that a lasted liner is stretched over a last (a pattern based on a foot shape) in the production process. This enhances the fit and durability of the boot liner. Since the liner materials are stretched in the lasting process, a significant amount of the compressibility is taken out of the liners. So, the fit of a lasted liner is truer in the long run than that of a sewn liner. Since the liner is stretched to an approximation of a foot shape, the initial feel is usually better than in a sewn liner. The firmer materials usually used in a lasted liner transmit foot steering motions more effectively and generally do not "pack out" as much as softer components. When the liner is removed from a boot shell, the differences between a lasted liner and a sewn liner can be observed as follows:

1. A lasted liner will have rounder corners.
2. The toe box will be higher and rounder in a sewn liner.
3. The forefoot area will be full in shape, overhanging the bottom of the lasted liner.
4. The heel cup is better defined in a lasted liner.
5. The seams on the bottom of a lasted liner will be protected by a firm sole cover on the bottom of the liner or by a tape.
6. The stitching in a lasted liner is generally tighter and heavier.
7. The liner materials are generally firmer in a lasted liner.

Injected Liners

Polyurethane-injected foam liners are the third type of boot liner. The first step in producing an injected liner involves sewing together the internal wicking sock. This internal lining is usually made of nylon and occasionally of loden wool. This internal sock is pulled over the inside mold or "plug," which represents the shape of a foot. An exterior mold closes over the plug, leaving a cavity over it and the sock. A polyurethane foam resin and catalyst are injected into the cavity and allowed to cure. The polyurethane foam adheres to the backing of the sock. The resulting foam liner is a firm, contoured replica of the boot shell and the planned foot shape.

Injected foam liners have less compressible material than either sewn or lasted liners. Advantages include significantly less "packing out" or growing of the liner with use, so the fit is truer with time. If a person has a protrusion on his or her foot which is inconsistent with the liner shape, the liner can be ground, sliced, or chemically softened with acetone to relieve pressure from the high point.

The less compressible injected foam has the disadvantage of forgoing the "automolding," or self-contouring, characteristics of the more compressible materials of either a sewn or lasted liner. An injected foam liner usually will wick moisture only as deep as the internal sock. So while it usually dries faster than a sewn or lasted liner, it has a wetter feel than liners that pull moisture deeper into their materials.

Sewn and lasted liners have a softer feel when a person first puts a boot on. In lasted liners, several manufacturers are adding layers of modern, high-tech insulating materials such as Thinsulate and Thermium.

Boot liners will probably wear out before boot shells. When liner materials wear out, the high points on the foot, such as the ankle bones, the heel, and the sixth toe, begin to take excess pressure. The life of the liner can be prolonged by adding new fit materials adjacent to the high spots.

If your liners become hard to live with, soaking them in a Woolite solution will help. Lysol spray will disinfect and freshen a pair of boot liners.

When custom fit is required on a pair of boots, the general rule is to start on the liner before shell alterations are performed. First add padding to the low points, then cut material from the high spots. Replacing a pair of liners is expensive, usually about half the cost of the boots, because of the intensive hand labor in production.

14 Foaming

In the search for a perfectly fitting ski boot, the proven method of foaming still offers one of the best possible approaches for containing the foot. When the foaming process is properly performed, it is a tool that can enhance performance as well as comfort.

Foaming is not difficult to do. It simply requires fulfilling a number of logical steps. But the omission of one step can take one of the best possible fit systems and turn it into one of the worst. Anyone fitting boots would be wise to follow a checklist during the foaming process to be sure that each step is done properly.

Skiers who have been involved in the sport for a number of years will recall the foam boots of the late 1960s and early 1970s. Although you may hear stories about how an early pair of foam boots provided the best fit an individual ever had, there are more anecdotes about how foamed boots broke down in a matter of days, or about skiers who fainted under the pressures and heat of the foaming process, or about foam pots that exploded.

Many of the early foam compounds had short shelf lives. If an out-of-date foam was used, the fit would break down extremely fast. Not all of the foam inner boots had adequate venting systems. Without them, gas pockets could develop, leaving a void in some portion of the bladder. Some of the early foams were quite brittle and quickly compressed.

About 1974, most foam systems were removed from the U.S. market. However, foam boots continued to be used in Europe, and through the late 1970s, foaming materials and processes used improved and refined. In 1980, a number of European boot producers brought the concept of foaming back across the Atlantic. Most serious boot fitting shops have offered it as an option since that time.

Modern foam materials are quite durable. If done properly, a modern foam innerboot will last longer than the equivalent nonfoam boot. If adequate airflow is established through the vent tubes before foaming, the likelihood of a gas pocket developing in the innerboot is almost nil. The performance and fit achieved in a foam boot make it a great option.

Preparing the Foam

Before foaming, the systems need to be prepared to assure a good reaction and flow of the foam and to provide room for the foot in critical areas of the boot. Foam materials must be stored at room temperatures. Freezing foam will usually destroy it. The foam components should be between 70 and 80 degrees Fahrenheit when injected. Above that temperature, the structure of the foam will be aerated, so the foam will be softer and will break down faster.

Below 70 to 80 degrees F, the catalytic action of the foam will be slow, and incomplete flow through the innerboot is likely. A meat thermometer can be used to judge the temperature of foam resin before injection.

When the foam ages, the material in the bottles crystallizes. If injected, these crystals can impede the flow of foam and may create hard spots in the fit. Boiling the foam materials prior to foaming dissolves the crystals and brings the foam back to a usable state.

Preparing the Boot

To begin, remove the innerboot from the boot shell. The foam enters from the tubes just above the heel, flows through the hollow envelope in the bladder, and exits through the tubes above the metatarsal heads (forefoot).

Inspect the tubes where they enter and exit the boot to be sure that they have not been flattened by their placement in the boot shells. The tubes

should be rounded all the way into the inner boot. Heating the flattened poly-tubing (with a heat gun or a hair dryer) will allow reshaping of the material.

When the foam is injected from the rear of the liner, it has a tendency to force the foot forward and to push the toes into the end of the toe box. A pair of thick neoprene toe cups placed on the feet will provide a cavity for the toes and assure an adequately large toe box after foaming.

In place of neoprene toe cups, two paper towels wadded and placed in the toe area of the innerboot will ensure that there is adequate room in the toe area after foaming. Of course, the material placed in the toe areas will make the boots feel much too small during foaming, but it is necessary for a good fit after the process is complete.

Flexion of the ankle joint causes a migration of the ankle bones through a range of travel about one centimeter in length. A cavity needs to be created in the foam liner to allow space for the ankle to be able to flex throughout this range. Place adhesive pads on the skier's ankles at least two centimeters larger than the circumference of the ankle bones.

Preparing the Foot

If a skier's foot pronates, it will migrate under weightbearing if the pronation is not controlled. Foaming creates a specific, static fit. If the foot migrates to and from the specific shape established in the foam, discomfort will occur. It is advisable to have a stabilized orthotic footbed before starting to foam a boot. If it is not possible to put the skier into a footbed, varus wedging and navicular pads should be used to secure a pronated foot.

Once the footbeds and toe box padding are in place, fit the innerboot back into the shell. With an overlap design, in a Tecnica or Rossignol boot, for example, the exit tubes should be pulled through the overlap of the shell above the forefoot and the exit tubes over the toes. With an open throat design, such as in a Sanmarco AXR or Raichle Flexon, cross the exit tubes over one another and exit the boot at both sides of the instep.

At this point, blow through the injection tubes at the back of the boot. Check if the air is coming out of the exit tubes to make sure there are no blockages.

Padding should be adhered to the foot over other problem bunions or sensitive areas to create hollows. Areas that commonly need padding are the back of the heel, the outer edge of the forefoot, and the instep.

A critical point in the foaming system is where the injection tubes fit over the hose barbs at the bottle cap. If a foaming accident is going to occur, it is most likely to involve the injection tube blowing off the hose barbs. As a precautionary measure, clamp the injection tubes onto the hose barbs with baling wire or plastic ratcheting trash bag ties.

Normally, it is best to foam without a ski sock on the foot because a small amount of compression will occur in the lining materials of the boot as it is used in skiing. After foaming, a sock can compensate for that compression. The exception is a person who has problems with the cold. A thin sock will allow additional volume for warmth.

Because of the close fit attained, foamed boots do have a tendency to be colder than their nonfoamed counterparts. Some boot fitters claim it helps to tape over the major blood flow areas of the foot. The layers of tape will create small channels in the foam promoting blood flow and warmth.

Most foaming kits come complete with a pair of polyethylene foot liners. Foam will creep through the seams of the innerboot during injection. These plastic liners keep the foot from becoming permanently attached to the innerboot. Once these plastic liners are on, it is time to put the feet into the boots.

Entering the Boot

At this point, the feeling in the boots is very uncomfortable. The toes are cramped, hard points are felt where the injection tubes enter and where the exit tubes leave the innerboot and the ankles and high points are squeezed by the padding. The feet will feel better in about 15 minutes, but, until then, it only gets worse.

When the foam is injected into the liner, extreme pressure is applied around the foot. The foot feels as if it is in a vise. Additionally, a good bit of heat is created by the catalytic reaction of the foam. This short period of discomfort is an investment in future comfort.

Before injecting the foam, the skier is placed in a stance where the toes are raised about 3 to 4 inches higher than the heels. This drives the foot back into the heel cup and reduces the possibility that the boot will be too short. Some fitters use handles that the skiers can pull down on to force themselves into the bottom and back of the boot. Putting on weighted vests to achieve the same end is not unheard of.

Close the collar buckles on the ski boot on a loose setting, then connect the buckles over the lower boot, but do not close them until the foam is injected.

When the skier is positioned on the foaming block, again blow through the injection tubes to assure clear flow through both the exit tubes. If air does not escape through both exit tubes, rotate the stopped-up tube 180 degrees in the boot liner and try again.

If there is still no success, and if the skier has a custom footbed, reduce the height of the footbed under the forefoot. Grind the boot board under the forefoot area to allow more volume at the exit tubes. Do not inject foam until some air can escape through both exit tubes. Only a minimal amount is required, so a restricted airflow is adequate.

Foaming the Boot

Make sure the foaming is done in a well-ventilated area. Gases emitted by the foam can cause health problems if the area is not properly vented.

Some companies have varying volumes of foam bottles for the different sizes of boots. Be sure to use the correct size, or even a larger size. Tape plastic bags to the exit tubes for the purpose of catching excess foam that flows through the system.

Remove the caps from one foam resin bottle and from a catalyst bottle. Combine the contents in the large resin bottle, screw the bottle onto the injection tubes, and then shake it. After shaking for 30 or 40 seconds, foam will begin to rise through the injection tubes.

Shortly after the foam enters the innerboot, the skier will begin to feel pressure around the ankles, the heel, and then the sides of the feet. Continue shaking the bottle vigorously until the foam is exiting both tubes. If the foam exits one tube first, pinch that tube to create back pressure, which will force foam through the opposite side of the boot and out the other tube.

After foam has escaped through both exit tubes, close the buckles over the lower section of the ski boot and drop the injection bottle. It is not a bad idea to place the bottle in a plastic bag in case of leakage. Then repeat the process on the second boot.

After the foam has been injected, have the skier stand still for about five minutes. During this period, the skier will think someone is attempting to separate his feet from the rest of his body by compression. (Having the skier bite a bullet or ski pole is often helpful during this period.)

After five minutes, the tubes can be pulled from the boots. Undo the buckles, grip the tubes with a pair of vise grips and pull straight out. When the tubes are pulled, excess gas escapes from the bladder and the viselike pressure dissipates.

Take off the boots, remove the pads from the ankles, and pull out the toe caps. Slide on a thin pair of ski socks and try the boots on again. Voila! If all of the steps have been completed successfully, the skier has a boot with a close, consistent fit.

If a hard spot develops somewhere in the liner after foaming, the foam can be softened and broken down by injecting acetone with a syringe into the the liner at that point. Padding and shell stretching can be done the same as for any conventional boot.

15 *Fitting Tools*

S killed craftsmen in any field agree that the quality of the work they produce is largely governed by the tools they use. Boot fitting is no exception.

There are a number of tools available to the boot fitter to make the task of fitting and repairing boots easier. Some of these are specifically designed for working with ski boots; others are generic tools with applications for boot work. They can be as basic as a slot screwdriver or as specialized as a boot spreader.

The most common repairs are replacing rivets in buckles or other attachments and stretching or expanding boot shells to obtain a better fit. In addition, grinding and sanding tools are used for a variety of fitting techniques. What follows are step-by-step procedures for using the basic tools for boot fitting and repair.

Riveting

The most common repair done on ski boots is rivet replacement. Buckles and other hardware are frequently damaged or torn from the boot while skiing or walking or when being transported. Occasionally, hinge rivets are separated from the lower boot shell.

If the rivet to be replaced attaches the buckle stand to the shell, a number of options are available to do the job. Pop riveters can be used to rivet a buckle back onto a boot shell. When the handle on a pop riveter is squeezed, it spreads the end of a pop rivet inside the boot by forcing the head of a finishing nail into the hollow rivet. A washer is fitted over the end of the rivet in the boot before using the tool. The head of the finishing nail expands the portion of the rivet inside the boot shell so it can no longer pass through the washer.

The most common buckle to be torn from a boot is the one closest to the toe. Attempting to rivet this forefoot buckle with most riveting tools requires athletic ability, dexterity, and a strong friend to spread the boot shell. A pop riveter, however, can insert the rivet from the exterior of the boot shell making the task much easier.

The most difficult part of pop riveting is fitting a washer over the interior end of the rivet. The pop rivets sup-

Rivet Pliers

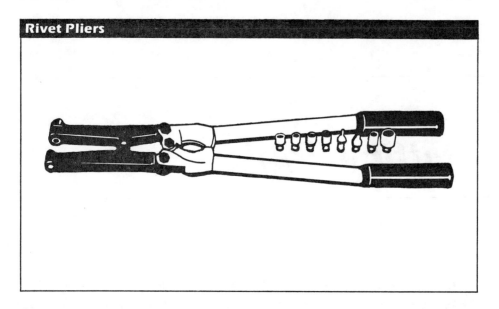

plied with commercial pop riveters are usually made of aluminum and are too soft for boot hardware applications. Use steel pop rivets, which are available from ski industry tool suppliers.

If the head of the pop rivet is not flattened over the washer, it can cause a nasty point of discomfort in a ski boot. A bit of additional flattening with a ballpeen hammer, or with a vise, is required to complete the job.

Rivet pliers also are a commonly used tool in boot repair. The long handles of a riveting pliers provide leverage so you can squeeze replacements for the original rivets into place or replace with two-part cap rivets.

One problem with rivet pliers is the difficulty in holding all the pieces while pressing the rivet in place with the pliers. It also is difficult to reach the forward recesses of a ski boot (especially a rear entry boot) with the riveting anvils—the heads that press the rivet. To simplify the first problem, hold the replacement buckle, rivet, and washer in place with duct or masking tape so your hands are free to work the riveting tool. A strong friend

or a Ski Tools boot spreader also makes it easier to reach the forward section of a boot with rivet pliers.

A boot press with a full complement of accessories includes riveting attachments. The most common use of a boot press is as a ball and ring boot stretcher. The major ski industry tool suppliers distribute boot presses as well as riveting anvils to work with those presses. The anvils come in small sizes to press the buckle and hardware rivets and in large sizes to press hinge rivets between the upper cuff and lower boot shell. The long arms of the boot press make it possible to press rivets into any portion of the boot shell.

Tecnica distributes a very effective riveting tool. The tool is delivered with numerous heads for various riveting operations. The anvil used on the interior of the boot shell for spreading the rivet has a recessed cavity that the washer rests in, leaving your hands free to operate the tool and hold the rivet in place.

For the large hinge rivets, the tool comes with a concave-shaped driver for rounded hinge rivets and a flat driver for flush hinge rivets. The tool includes a slotted anvil that meshes with the teeth of a wire form bale block. (The bale block is the slotted piece that front entry buckles usually attach to on the arch side of the boot.)

An alternative to replacing a rivet is using a "T-Nut." A T-Nut is a flat plate with a threaded shaft that is placed inside the ski boot in the rivet hole. A pan head or flat head machine screw, or Allen screw, is fitted through the buckle, or hardware item to be attached, and is threaded into the T-Nut. Locktite should be placed on the threads when using a T-Nut to adhere the screw so it will not vibrate loose.

Heat Gun

Shell Expansion

When a skier has a bump, knob or other foot problem that is inconsistent with the shape of the ski boot shell, the shell often has to be stretched or expanded to accommodate the foot's shape. To expand a boot shell, locate the exact spot where the shell needs enlarging. Slowly heat the shell until the plastic is malleable. Expand the shell using a stretching tool, and then allow it to cool.

Four methods are used to heat a boot shell for expansion. The most common tool used is the industrial heat gun. The heat gun used most often for boot expansion has a 300 to 500 degree heating element. A vent on the side of the heat gun is opened to allow more air to pass over the element, creating a range of temperatures. It is best to use this tool at the lower end of its temperature range for shell expansion.

Patience is a must when heating a boot shell. A short blast of heat should be applied and then allowed to penetrate for 20 or 30 seconds before applying the next blast of heat. Use caution, and do not overheat the shell's exterior.

Boiling the boot shell using a crock pot or a large kettle is a common method of heating a shell for expansion. When boiling a shell, be careful not to heat the boot sole or it may be distorted in the stretching process, destroying its compatibility with a ski binding.

The Tool Company of New Hampshire and Sidas supply infrared shell heaters. These heaters utilize heating elements on goosenecks that can be placed over a section of the shell. A timer is set, and the plastic is slowly and thoroughly warmed.

Another tool used for heating boot shells is a heat lamp. The heat lamp is usually set on a timer so that it shuts off at the proper time. It is placed 5 or 6 inches over the appropriate spot on the boot shell and turned on to heat the plastic.

After heating the boot shell, there are two types of tools commonly used to expand the shell—the boot press and the Superfit expander. The boot press was mentioned earlier as a riveting tool. It is a dual purpose device. For shell expansion, an expansion head is usually placed on the lower arm of the boot press. That arm is placed in the boot shell, positioning the expansion head at the exact point where the shell expansion needs to be performed.

A ring, with a larger diameter than the corresponding stretching head, is placed on the upper arm of the press. Pulling the control lever on the press forces the ring over the expansion head and presses out the boot shell.

The Superfit expander uses a hydraulic pump that forces an expansion head against the interior of the shell. There are several options for expansion with this system. The interior of one side of the shell can be pushed from the opposite side of the shell with the two-caliper expander. A foot-shaped device can be placed in a boot to force a specific point. Or, the Superfit expander can be purchased with a C-ring which allows a head to be driven into the ring to expand a specific point.

After expanding the boot shell, the plastic is cooled. Cooling can be done by leaving the boot on the stretcher for 30 minutes or more so the shell cools slowly. For faster cooling, water can be poured over the stretched shell or ice can be packed on it.

Hand Grinding Tools

Hand grinding tools should be treated with respect. In boot fitting, they are used to grind away the exterior of polyurethane foam innerboots or to grind the interior plastic of a boot shell to relieve pressure points. With a carbide burr, a hand grinding tool can remove rivets or other hardware items from the boot.

Probably the best known of these tools is the Dremel eighth-inch shank variable speed Moto-tool. It is a hobbyist's tool for sculpting, cutting, shaping, or reducing materials. The Dremel has a light duty motor that is adequate for occasional use in a ski shop. The eighth-inch shank limits the size of carbide grinding bits that can be used to only smaller-sized bits.

Makita, Dayton, Craftsman, and other manufacturers produce quarter-inch die grinders that hold up well for everyday use in a ski shop. The heavier motor in these tools provides good power for grinding and cutting and will last longer than the eighth-inch grinders. Larger carbide-tipped burrs are readily available in a quarter-inch shaft.

The larger burrs cut faster, maintain their edge for a longer period of time, and leave smoother surfaces. The disadvantage of quarter-inch die grinders is the difficulty in getting these tools into the toe areas and small recesses of a ski boot.

Foredom and Dremel manufacture flexible shaft grinding tools. Like a dentist's drill, the grinding head of these tools is on a flexible extension that can be fitted into small nooks and crannies. This offers some important advantages in removing a rivet from the forward section of the boot, in grinding out the toe area, or in contouring a boot board foundation in the front of a shell. The Foredom flexible shaft grinder has replaceable collets so the shank size can be adapted for grinding burrs of various shaft sizes.

Sanding

Finishing custom footbeds (orthotics), reducing boot boards, thinning insoles, beveling fit aids, and some liner work require use of a sander. Most shops have a wet belt sander used for ski tuning. The same machine can be used with the water pump turned off for boot work. A coarse belt should be designated as the exclusive belt for boot work.

It is not a good idea to use the same belt for ski tuning that is used for boot work. Urethane foams, neoprene, and adhesives picked up by the belt from boot work will not enhance the glide characteristics of skis tuned on the boot work belt.

A drum sander is a nice device for boot sanding operations. It can perform clean bevels down the sides of a part and will create flat surfaces under a footbed. A drum sander does not have the nasty habit of tearing the piece from your hand and tossing it across the room as a belt sander may do.

A small platen sander can create a flat surface on the bottom of a posted footbed. It is a good tool for flattening the boot board from under the innerboot to mesh properly with the footbed.

Hand Tools

Every workstation in a boot fitting shop must be equipped with a number of hand tools. Canting, forward lean, and flex adjustments require various slot screwdrivers, Phillips-head and Posidrive screwdrivers, and metric Allen wrenches.

Various types of vise grips are very handy for boot work. Standard vise grips are often needed to hold screws, T-Nuts, rivets, hardware items, and buckle parts. They also do a good job of crimping when replacing the heel-instep adjustment cable on a rear entry boot.

Needle-nose vise grips are useful in pulling obstinate innerboots from rear entry shells. Duckbill vise grips help in stretching broad areas of plastic and are good for gripping buckles without leaving teeth marks in the paint.

A razor knife and a seam ripper allow you to enter a boot liner to remove padding or stiffening material that may be causing the skier discomfort. After opening a liner, you must reseal it with Aquaseal (a neoprene glue) or Velcro (when opening a nylon innerboot like Raichle or Lange) or by sewing with an awl, an upholstery tool. Thread is fed through the needle of the awl. When the needle is driven through a boot liner, the sliced area can be closed up by using a mattress stitch.

Needle-nose pliers are often required for getting into small areas in the innerboot or shell. Channel locks are not often used in boot work but are ideal for opening sticky glue bottles.

The tool department of a good quality hardware store can supply tools that will save hours of work. Boot fitting is a creative task. Medical supply houses have many neat little tools used in surgery that have great applications in boot fitting. Medical tools are expensive, but the right tool is usually worth the cost.

There are many ways to use tools to save time and frustration. An investment in good-quality tools is an essential first step for any shop hoping to produce quality work in solving boot problems for skiers.

16 *Repairing Boot Buckles*

At first glance, repairing closure systems on ski boots seems like a simple project. Twenty years ago, it was. Today, boot manufacturers have developed many closure systems that improve performance and aid in foot containment. It is the diversity in systems that has vastly complicated repairs.

Closure systems are broken down into two major groups: external buckling mechanisms and internal retention devices. Within these groups, there are almost as many systems as there are boot brands. Repairing them is a daily chore for any area ski shop.

It is impossible to list every model and brand of boot on the market today with a specific repair method, so only the most common closure problems are identified here.

External Buckling Systems

Wireform systems are found on many traditional racing ski boots. These systems have a formed wire bale on a buckle which anchors into a bale block and draws the halves of an overlap boot shell together. Several sizes of wire forms or bales are available for these boots to improve the fit.

To replace a wire form, simply spread the base of the wire, freeing it from the buckle. If a wire form is difficult to remove by hand, a pair of pliers will make it easier. Tape the jaws of the pliers with duct tape to avoid scuffing the wire forms.

The base of the wire form on most boots adjusts by screwing it on a threaded shaft. To remove this threaded base from the shaft, first remove the tiny "C" clip from the end of the shaft. The wire form base can then be twisted off the shaft easily.

The most common failure with these buckles is a broken threaded shaft. In this case, the easiest repair is to replace the buckle assembly at the shell. These buckles are held in place with two press fit rivets.

To remove a buckle, drill off the heads of the rivets, or grind them off with a die grinder. New rivets are needed which will go through the buckle stand, the boot shell, and a washer inside the boot's interior.

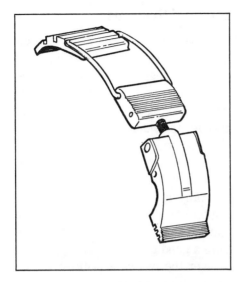

The base of the rivet is peened (flattened) over the interior washer. The easiest way to attain this peening is with a rivet tool. An inexpensive pop riveter can be purchased at any hardware store. If you do not have this tool, flatten the rivet with a ballpeen hammer.

Pop rivets do a good job of holding a buckle in place. When using pop rivets on the interior of the boot shell, use a washer to prevent the rivets from tearing out.

An alternative to riveting is a T-Nut, a threaded cylinder on a flat base. The base fits in the boot shell with the shaft protruding into the hole in the boot shell. A small pan-head bolt is driven through the buckle stand into the threaded T-Nut. Use mechanics' Locktite on the threads to prevent loosening of the bolt with use.

If a buckle or bale block is torn out of the boot, inspect the holes the rivets were torn from. If any small tears are present, drill a new hole that is larger than the tear. Use a large washer or T-Nut when reattaching the buckle to prevent it from tearing out again.

The bale block, on the opposite side of the boot shell from the buckle, is occasionally torn from the shell. The buckle block is held in place by a rivet or has a rivet-type shaft integrated into the bale block. As with the buckle replacement, the base of the rivet is peened over a washer on the interior of the boot shell.

Ratchet strap buckles are the most common type of external buckling systems on new boots. These have a nylon strap with teeth that mesh with a spring-loaded clasp on the opposite side of the boot shell.

Many of these systems have extra straps available in various sizes. If a ratchet strap is broken, simply push the remaining part of the strap toward its base to free it from the buckle.

If the buckle is damaged or torn from the boot shell, use the same riveting method described earlier. The clasp on the opposite side of the shell is held in place with one rivet in most cases. If the clasp stand has been bent or deformed, the action of the ratchet strap will be impaired. Trim the sides of the ratchet strap to improve its sliding ability.

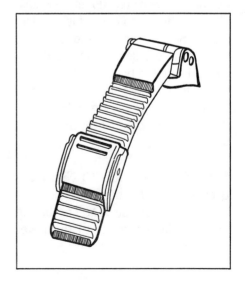

Braided steel cables coated in nylon are used extensively in external buckling systems. They come in two forms: (1) a cable attached to one side of the boot and a buckle on the opposite side; and (2) a cable integrated into the buckle which loops onto a nub on the opposite side of the boot when closing.

In the first, if the metal end of the cable is deformed, it is difficult to disengage the cable end from the buckle. A little reshaping with a pair of pliers can bring the cable back to shape and keep it from hanging up in the buckle teeth. If the cable is too deformed or breaks, it needs replacement.

A U-shaped hook is commonly used to fasten the cable to the molding on the boot shell. This hook can be removed by prying with a screwdriver or pulling it with some chain-nose pliers. Fit the new cable into the retainer and squeeze it back over the molding on the boot shell.

The second cable system is integrated into the buckle. A new buckle must be riveted to the shell if the cable is broken.

Some boots have a tab-and-slot buckle system on upper buckles. These require no tools for replacement. Simply slide the buckle and ratchet strap assembly toward the inside edge of the boot, and the assembly is free. There are two different locations for the buckle to be placed depending on the size of the skier's leg.

The lower cable attaches to the front of the boot with a T-Nut, loops over the top of the foot, and then screws into the buckle. The buckle over the instep rivets to the lower shell under the upper cuff.

Internal Systems

Most rear entry boots have an internal retention system with a cable over the instep region. If this cable breaks, it usually requires crimping a new cable into place. The cable is fed through the sides of the boot, through the adjustment lever, over the pressure distribution plate, and into the crimping tube.

Crimping can be done with a crimping tool or a pair of vise grips. Crimp the cable in several locations to assure a good grip. If the crimping tube is over the pressure plate, it will require some shaping.

Some models have instep cables that attach on one end to an adjustment dial. Feed in loops through the boot shell, then over the instep, and then rivet to the inner shell.

Most forefoot adjustments in rear entry boots involve a screw mechanism. To prevent accidental disassembly of such a system, the end is often peened to prevent the nut from passing over the end of the bolt. To disassemble these forefoot adjustments, grind the peening off the end of the internal bolt with a grinding tool. Then unscrew the device to disassemble it. Reassembly of these devices usually requires patience and persistence (and small hands). A pair of channel locks, needle-nose pliers, or chain-nose vise grips will help assemble these parts.

Broken closure systems are often caused by an individual who overstresses the systems on a boot. This means the skier is in need of additional fitting materials in the boot. Some Snugs Flopacs, wraparound pads, narrowing pads, insoles, or molded footbeds will reduce the stress on the system.

17 *Boot Orthotics*

Skiers looking for maximum performance and improved comfort from their ski boots are replacing their stock footbeds or insoles with customized "orthotics" that match the shape of the bottom of the foot exactly. The customized footbed fills voids and gives the foot an intimate, supportive foundation.

Although individuals with significant foot instabilities gain the most benefit from a customized footbed, all skiers will see an improvement in fit and comfort. As with any customized touch, the skier pays a price for added comfort and performance. But since they were first introduced in the 1970s, customized footbeds have made enough skiers happy to justify the added investment.

Most off-the-shelf footbeds range in price from as low as $10 to about $30 at retail. Shop-customized footbeds, depending on the system, typically cost the skier from $35 to $125. "Posted" or stabilized footbeds (footbeds returned to a lab for finishing) will cost from about $70 to $125 if ordered through a ski shop.

A good customized footbed, depending on the system used, will last an average skier from about 100 ski days to 300 or more. A cork customized footbed offers the longest wear.

Customized footbeds can be removed from old boots and installed in new ones, usually with a minimum of reshaping. It is not necessary to order new footbeds when switching to new boots.

Most ski boot manufacturers like to believe their boots provide all the comfort and performance necessary without modifications or additions. But they also concede that with the endless variety of feet their boots are expected to fit, a customized footbed can be a good idea. They also know that anything that can be done to improve the fit will help make a contented customer who might just stay with the same brand when it comes time to buy a new pair.

Boot makers recommend a customized footbed, particularly if the skier is going to a custom foam fit boot. The footbed can enhance comfort, and the foot should be supported before the boot is foamed around it. Some boot suppliers recommend that their top-of-the-line custom boots should be sold with a custom orthotic to get the optimum performance out of the boot.

Most skiers notice that subtle foot steering movements are enhanced with the addition of footbeds. For example, hard, chattery snow is easier to contend with. Corrective materials under some footbeds minimize foot instabilities, improving power as well as comfort. And a good footbed minimizes fatigue in the feet and legs.

There are a number of systems available today for fabricating custom footbeds. There are also several insoles available which are not custom molded but are attempts at mass-produced, off-the-shelf support systems.

Most custom footbed systems use a heat moldable plastic material, which is contoured to the shape of the foot. Most use a foam casting pillow as the contouring device. Using the "pillow" system to shape the footbed, the hot, malleable footbed "blank" is placed on the casting pillow. The skier stands on the warm blank, forming it to the shape of the foot. The blank cools while the skier remains stationary. Then this reverse image cast of the foot is trimmed to fit in the ski boot.

Often, materials are laminated to the bottom of the cast and ground flat to add stability to the device. This stabilizing material may be ground into a wedge to improve the fit of the ski boot and to minimize excessive pronation of the foot.

The Superfeet System

The noticeable exception to the foam casting pillow is the Superfeet system. Superfeet utilizes a heat mold-able cork system. While being cast, the skier is seated in an elevated chair with the feet hanging free.

The footbed blank and stabilizing materials are placed in a stirrup in their warm, molten state. Then the stirrup is attached to the foot with elastic straps. Hoses from a vacuum pump are placed under the straps. A plastic bag is fitted over the entire paraphernalia. The vacuum pump draws the footbed blank into the contours of the unweighted foot. After the footbed cools, it is trimmed to the interior of the ski boot. The advantage Superfeet offers is firm support, positive rear foot stabilization, and a durable footbed.

At a lower price, Superfeet has the "Vac Advantage" footbed that is molded with a plastic-based core and foam upper. Superfeet also has an off-the-shelf footbed called the Energizer, which is a lower-priced introductory option.

The Peterson System

Peterson is the largest distributor of moldable plastic footbeds for ski boots. They offer a wide variety of footbed options that range from a pre-cast off-the-shelf support up to a sport orthotic that is stabilized in their orthotic laboratory to biomechanically improve the position of the foot. The skier receives significantly more benefit the farther up the Peterson line the skier elects to go.

Peterson casting stands are available in various degrees of sophistication, depending on the level of training of the technician casting the footbeds. If the shop is building a full ski orthotic, Peterson offers a stance alignment system. This system employs knee cups and plumb bobs to properly position the anatomy of the lower leg and foot. Less sophisticated footbeds require less equipment.

The ski orthotic utilizes a polyethylene base with a nylon sheathed foam top skin. After casting the blank (or core), it is usually shipped back to the Peterson laboratory, where the device is "posted" or stabilized. This footbed offers extremely good shaping, durability, and performance.

Peterson's Bioski with radial support uses a harder plastic blank. The footbed is cast, trimmed to the ski boot, then stabilized with a horseshoe-shaped support under the arch and heel area. This approach provides a fairly stable device for about half the cost of the ski orthotic. It is not as exact and does not offer as much mechanical correction as a ski orthotic.

The Comfort Ski is a basic hard plastic cast with a foam top surface. It is not a stabilized device. It will improve comfort and reduce fatigue in a ski boot. Since it is not a stabilized device, a person with an unstable foot will not find it as effective in improving performance as the Bioski or ski orthotic. It does offer cost savings.

Peterson also offers an off-the-shelf insole for a lower-priced introductory system.

The Boot Lab System

The Boot Lab system has a unique casting pillow. The heated footbed blank is placed on a bladder that will be filled with air. While the skier is standing on the warm blank, the air system forces the blank into the contours and cavities of the foot, providing excellent shaping. The Boot Lab blank employs a heat-moldable plastic base with a heat-contouring closed-cell foam top surface.

The Boot Lab offers the option of sending the cast to their laboratory for biomechanical corrections or the noncorrected device can be trimmed and fit directly into the ski boot. As with the Peterson system, the laboratory-corrected device should offer better performance and fit.

The Boot Lab has recently developed a foam, moldable footbed. The foam system is often warmer and more easily stabilized than plastic devices.

The Sidas System

Sidas footbed systems, distributed by Rossignol, offer a number of footbed options. At the top of their line is the VAS Bio. This highly shock-absorbent material will reduce pounding stresses experienced in the bumps and hard snow.

The Sidas PolyDorane is a firm footbed blank created specifically for alpine skiing. It is a thin profile, nonstabilized device with a closed-cell foam top surface. It requires slightly more time in casting for the material to set than the material used by some other companies. The additional flexibility it offers relative to the hard plastics used in most footbeds is preferred by some skiers.

The Sidas Basic is a pared-down version of the PolyDorane. It is a lighter-weight, more flexible footbed. These characteristics make it a good choice for cross-country skiing or telemarking.

The Biopro and the Lite footbed blanks round out the Sidas line. The Biopro is a double density foam system. The foam is a good antivibration material for a person who would like a dampened feeling in the boot. The Lite, made of Dureen, Thermofelt, and a material Sidas calls Thermaflex, is a lightweight, flexible footbed, good for cross-country and running applications.

The Sidas Casting Stand can be supplied with a pedoscope and a pedograph. The pedoscope is a layer of glass the footbed candidate stands on. Several inches under the glass is a mirror. The bottom of the foot is examined under weight bearing with this device. It gives the footbed technician the opportunity to observe places where the weight is focused and where there is the potential for pressure discomforts. The pedograph is a membrane placed over the pedoscope on which the impression of a person's footprint is left. Back lighting shows the location of pressure points. The pedograph gives a good indication of alignment problems.

Sidas does not offer laboratory services. Most Sidas footbeds are fit without corrective posting.

The Biodynamics System

Biodynamics, distributed by the Tool Company of New Hampshire, is very similar to the Sidas system. The casting stand uses a rubber dome system for shaping the footbed blanks. The Biodynamic blank called Bio-soles uses a foam, thermal plastic lamination. It is a very low profile footbed with a wide heel area for cupping.

Most footbeds remove volume, snugging the boot significantly. If extra space is nonexistent in your boots, either the Biodynamics or Sidas footbeds are probably the best choices.

Dynamic Foam Products

Dynamic Foam Products of Steamboat Springs, Colorado, is producing a very user friendly footbed. The footbed blank utilizes five layers of thermal sensitive foams. It heats to a malleable casting temperature much faster than most other blanks and sets much more quickly, too.

The lamination of five material layers minimizes distortion of the blank in the heating and casting process. Dynamic Foam Products will supply a basic casting pillow, but the blanks can be used with any other casting stand.

After the skier's foot impression has been captured in the Dynamic Foam Products footbed blank, the footbed is sanded to fit the boot and to provide biomechanical stability. Because of the type of foams used and the nature of the footbed configuration, this system is much faster and easier to post, or wedge for pronation problems, than other footbed systems. Skiers who have tried the Dynamic Foam Products footbed claim it is one of the warmest of the footbeds.

The Biotech System

The Biotech footbed, sold by Technology and Tools in Bondville, Vermont, features a sculpted footbed blank. The footbed uses a firm plastic base, with a nylon-covered neoprene top surface.

The forefoot region of the plastic base is thinned. When the footbed is heated and cast, the thinner forefoot region warms deeply, providing excellent forefoot shaping.

The Biotech footbeds can be returned to Technology and Tools for laboratory posting. A simpler radial heel support is also available for minimal stabilizing.

The Biotech casting stand is a simple nylon covered angled foam pillow between two platforms. It provides very deep heel cupping.

The Ultra-Fit System

Foot Image Technology of Bend, Oregon, may be revolutionizing the footwear industry by using computers to match feet to the appropriate shape of footwear. Thirty-one different measurements and observations are employed in directing boot customers to what they believe to be the most suitable boot.

One of the recommendations the computer may give us is for footbeds. The computer is programmed to mesh with whatever footbed system the shop is using, recommending the correct footbed blank for a given application.

Foot Image Technology has their own footbed system called the Ultra-Fit footbed system, which uses a dome somewhat like the Sidas casting domes. The major distinction is that the two Foot Image Technology domes are independent, allowing variations in spread for differing anatomical structures.

The Ultra-Fit footbed utilizes a thermoplastic base with a foam upper. It is somewhat thinner than most other footbed blanks but more rigid than the Sidas PolyDorane, thereby offering more extreme stabilization.

The Ultra-Fit footbed is keyed with a mark to assist in positioning it properly on the casting domes. The Ultra-Fit can be used as a noncorrective device or can be stabilized with add-on foams.

Two additional footbed blanks are available from Foot Image Technology —the Ultra-Foam and Ultra-Light. The Ultra-Foam is a three-quarter-length posted footbed with its major application in flexible footwear such as running shoes. The Ultra-Light is a device that can be varied in thickness and flexibility. A competent technician can build a custom device with the Ultra-Light to deal with varying problems and specific needs either for rigidity or giving compression.

The art of development of customized footbeds is still in its youth. Several significant innovations have taken place in the past year. More improvements are on the horizon. It has only been recently that most ski shops have acquired footbed fabricating equipment.

The Ortho-Tech system distributes a laboratory-fabricated footbed system utilizing hard plastic devices. These devices are very durable and reduce the amount of in-shop knowledge that is required to produce the orthotic since actual fabrication is done by experts in the lab.

The ski shop makes a cast of the foot using a compressible foam block. Information about the skier and the skier's foot is sent along with the cast to the laboratory where the footbed is constructed. After the footbeds are completed, they are returned to the ski shop.

With more use, the quality of the products available will continue to improve, promising skiers concerned with performance even more options.

18 Answers to the Most Common Boot Questions

The same questions about ski boots and how to fit them are asked over and over. It seems to be a topic that is most important to skiers of all abilities. From a boot fitter's point of view, the questions are usually basic.

Bob Gleason, owner of the Boot Doctor's shop in Taos, New Mexico, is a consultant to ski boot manufacturers and has been teaching workshop classes for boot technicians for twelve years. These are the questions most often asked by ski shop personnel attending his workshops and by customers in his shop. Gleason readily admits that the answers to most questions are not as "black and white" as skiers would like them to be.

1. How long will a pair of boots last?
Typically, a ski boot will last for about 150 days of skiing, but that depends on several factors. A large, muscular skier will usually apply more stress to a boot than an average-size skier. The stress will speed the softening of the boot shell. As a boot gets soft, especially medially and laterally, power and quickness to the ski are sacrificed. A large, strong skier can overflex a boot, leading to breakage. The liner will compress faster, and comfort will be sacrificed prematurely.

A lightweight skier or a person who skis with a very light touch can get many more than the average number of days out of a pair of boots. I have seen boots with more than 250 days of use which were in good serviceable condition. Bump skiing and racing are hard on boots and wear them out more quickly than cruising.

Walking in boots can destroy them in short order. Ski patrollers who regularly hike bombing routes can render a pair of boots unsafe in 30 to 40 days of use. Extreme moisture and continual use without drying will cause liner materials to rot and break down. Drying liners too quickly and under too much heat can cause liner materials to shrink and crack or, in some cases, melt.

2. How can you tell when a boot is worn out?
The most obvious sign of a worn out boot is a badly worn boot sole. If the glide area of the boot sole (the surface

that interfaces with the antifriction plate on most bindings) becomes pocked or badly worn, binding release may be compromised.

A worn boot sole may rock, twist, or torque in a binding system causing uneven contact pressure. This will result in compromised retention and release. Mechanical testing of the boot/ binding system will point up boot incompatibility in this situation.

Broken hardware is often a sign of boot rigor mortis. When a buckle or other functional piece of hardware fatigues to the point of breakage, other components of the boot seem to follow close behind. Broken boot buckles are often an indicator that the boot liner has compressed to the point where the skier has to overload the closure in an attempt to secure the foot.

The boot liner is usually the first component of a boot to wear out. When hard spots begin to develop at physical high points (such as ankle bones), it could indicate that the foam fit materials adjacent to that spot have compressed. (Most boot liners have several layers of foam cut and laminated together in a shape similar to the reverse image of a foot.)

Squeeze the liner and feel for resiliency in the foam fit materials. If the liveliness of the foam is spent, the liner will not be comfortable. Seams coming apart, cracks in the liner material or interior fit packs, curling and peeling of liner components, and progressive discomfort all indicate liner death.

Shell degradation is usually subtler. The boot becomes softer with use. Because it is a gradual process, the skier is usually unaware that the performance of the boot is suffering. As the boot gets softer, it becomes difficult for the skis to hold an edge in hard and chattery conditions. The skier has a tendency to lose balance forward, over the tips of his skis. Through the finish of the turn, it becomes more difficult to recover, and the skier loses balance to the rear. Loss of balance and edge control are the indicators of a boot shell's declining integrity.

3. Should a ski boot hurt?

The answer to this question is unequivocally no, not in the act of skiing. It is true that a boot should not fit like a sneaker. The foot and lower leg need to be firmly contained in the hard plastic confines of a ski boot. Firm containment is necessary to effectively pressure and direct a ski.

A properly fitted ski boot does not have a soft, cushy feeling. It has a firm, solid, consistent feeling. Good boot fitting implies stabilizing the foot first. Then the interior dimensions of the boot are sculpted through the addition and deletion of material and reshaping components until the boot reflects a reverse image of the skier's foot.

Pain is a result of either an improper matching of the boot to the foot (points of high contact and areas of low contact) or instability (causing the foot to migrate from its proper location in the boot). There may be mechanical problems in a boot which cause pain. If the boot flexes above or below the point where the skier's ankle flexes, pain can result. If components of the boot migrate, causing a focus of pressure at specific areas during flexion, they can cause pain. On these occasions, the functional operation of the boot needs to be altered.

A properly fitted ski boot is like a bear hug. You are aware of the pressure and shape of the person hugging you. But a hug never hurts.

4. If the boot does not hurt, should I make changes?

Even if a boot does not hurt, performance often can be enhanced and potential fit problems can be avoided. A look at the foot, weighted and unweighted, reveals to a good boot fitter the alignment changes that can cause pressure problems and instabilities that hinder performance. An excessively pronated foot (a foot that flattens under weight bearing) will be under continual motion while skiing.

Under the right conditions, that motion will eventually lead to discomfort. The continual motion of a foot pronating each time weight is applied to it rapidly stretches a boot liner, speeding the process of liner breakdown. Adding support under a pronated foot in the form of a custom footbed or through applying wedges and navicular pads will increase the life expectancy of the boot.

High points on the foot should be isolated. As a boot liner compresses with use, the high points are the first areas to suffer. Filling the voids adjacent to high spots is good problem-preventing practice. A boot that is too large (as most boots are) may feel cushy, but its performance will be poor.

Start the fitting process by measuring the foot and comparing that measurement to the size of the boot. A boot that is too large will perform better after it is packed with dense fitting materials.

Usually a boot's performance can be enhanced through the functional adjustments on the boot. This includes tuning the cant for an individual, setting the flex based on an individual's size, ability, and skiing preferences, and setting the forward lean.

5. What is better, a front entry or rear entry boot?

This is one of the great ski industry debates. Of course, the answer is neither. The key is not whether the boot closes in front or in back but how a particular boot and its closure mechanism matches the shape and biomechanics of the individual's foot. In other words, the most important considerations are how it fits and whether that particular boot model functions properly.

Wide feet can only be comfortable in boots that offer enough volume to accommodate them. Narrow feet will find much better skiing performance and comfort in boots narrow enough to adequately contain that low volume structure without distorting the boot (front entry) or divorcing the foot from the boot's structural shell (rear entry).

A foot with a high instep (top of the foot) not only needs a boot with enough volume to allow for that instep but a closure system that can apply pressure to areas around the instep rather than directly downward on the instep. With current technology, there is no one boot or closure system that adapts to all foot shapes. The introduction of numerous rear entry designs in the past ten years has led to some innovative closure systems. These systems have improved both rear entry and front entry boots.

6. What does canting do?

Canting simply matches the shape of the boot shaft to the shape of the individual's leg. In most cases, when properly canted, the center of the individual's knee mass will locate over the skier's second toe (the one next to the big toe) when the boot's sole is flat.

If the skier is bowlegged, the boots will be resting on their outside edges when the skier is standing in a natural stance. To stand on a flat ski or to place the ski on edge, the bowlegged skier forces his or her knees together, compensating by skiing with the knees tucked together (extreme A-frame). These skiers have a tendency to catch outside edges and suffer stress and strain in the knees. They are poor gliders since it is difficult for them to ride a flat ski. They frequently cross their ski tails. Tipping the boot's shaft outward (positive canting) or raising the inside edge of the boot sole will relieve these skiing problems.

The opposite problem is experienced by the knock-kneed skier. When standing in a natural stance, this skier's boots will be tipped onto the inside edge of the boot soles. To flatten the boots and ride a flat ski or to reduce edge contact, the skier will ski with knees apart. This skier is continually overedging.

It is difficult for knock-kneed skiers to be light and supple. Their tendency is to bounce and chatter through the turns and the inside edges of their ski tips are often chipped and worn. Knock-kneed individuals catch inside edges and do more than their share of face plants. They cross their tips frequently. They are slow gliders and often find themselves in an unintentional wedge or snowplow.

This skier's boot shafts need to be tipped inward (negative cant), or the outer edge of the boot sole should be raised. With most canting tools, adjustments are made to the boot which will move the center of the knee over the second toe when the boot sole is flat.

7. What will a footbed do for me?

Many serious skiers have become aware of custom footbeds (orthotic devices). After skiing with a properly constructed footbed, it is difficult to consider ever skiing without one. A custom footbed provides the foundation for correct fit in a ski boot. It provides a platform that improves balance, tactile sensitivity, and comfort.

The bottom of the foot is the primary area to be fitted. Problems around the sides of the foot, top of the foot, in the toe box, and in the lower leg will be reduced when the bottom of the foot is fitted properly. As when building a house, the foundation must be stable or the walls and roof will crack and fall.

A well-built footbed reduces excessive motion and migration of the foot inside a ski boot. When the foot is held in a constant position, the boot fitter can shape the rest of the boot to the image of the foot.

Most people's feet are pronated. That means their feet flatten somewhat when weight is applied. The forefoot rotates outward (duck-footed), the ankles tip inward, and the lower leg rotates toward the inside. The foot elongates and the arch stretches. When walking barefoot or in a pliable pair of shoes, pronation allows the foot to contour to the surfaces the foot is standing on. Pronation provides shock absorption at heel strike when an individual is walking.

While skiing, you generally do not have heel strike—or toe off—as in walking. Rather the foot is in a mid-stance position. So a ski footbed is fabricated to contour to the surfaces underfoot in a set position. A properly constructed footbed reduces foot pronation, creating a firmer structure.

If the foot performs as a firm structure rather than as a pliable shock absorber, it is better at applying pressure. When the foot is better at applying pressure, the skier is quicker edge to edge, is more powerful, and has better balance.

A footbed reduces the outward flare of the forefoot, the elongation of the arch, and the inward tipping and twisting of the ankle and lower leg, so the foot and leg align better with the shape of a rigid plastic ski boot. The result is a far more comfortable fit.

Even if a skier's foot is not pronated, a custom footbed offers a number of benefits. A footbed matches the shape of the bottom of the foot exactly. It spreads pressures intimately across the entire surface of the bottom of the foot. An individual with a stable (nonpronated) foot will generally have high contact at the inside and outside balls of the feet and under the heel.

This contact can cause numbness under the toes and in the forefoot and a feeling of fatigue in the feet after standing for long periods. By spreading pressures across the entire bottom of the foot, a footbed reduces contact pressures and greatly improves comfort.

8. Why do my feet always get cold?
Free blood flow is the key ingredient in warmth. The body burns calories in its central core to generate heat. Blood flowing from the body's core carries heat to the extremities. The body prioritizes where the heat should go.

We possess the "mammalian dive reflex." This physiological instinct allows the body to survive long periods of exposure to the cold by retaining heat in the important functional organs of the body at the expense of our extremities. In other words, if your body is cold, it draws heat from the arms, legs, hands, and feet to keep the internal organs warm.

A key to keeping the feet warm is to dress the entire body warmly. The brain is an important internal organ. If a skier does not wear a hat when skiing, a tremendous amount of the body's heat will be lost through the head. As a result, the feet will be cold.

If the torso is not adequately layered, the body will limit the heat passed to the feet and cold will result. On the way to the feet, the blood covers a significant distance through the legs. If the legs are not well insulated, heat will be shed enroute to the feet. Skiing in blue jeans will assure cold feet.

Ski boots fit for optimum performance will be quite constrictive. On a cold day, a skier should undo the buckles or closure mechanisms whenever not skiing (on lifts, in long lift lines, while walking, at lunch). That way blood can flow more freely to and from the foot for better warmth.

Clothing items in the boot can severely restrict blood flow. Only one good pair of ski socks should be worn. Two pairs will have a tendency to bunch and restrict blood flow. Socks for skiing should be of a hydrophobic material (wool, silk, polypro, Thermax). Cotton and many synthetics hold moisture (hydrophilic), chilling the skin.

Socks collect oils and salts from the skin. These factors will reduce their ability to wick. Dirty socks will be cold. In-the-boot ski pants and stirrups from stretch pants will create bands of constriction that will cause restrictions in blood flow. With in-the-boot pants, snow and moisture will spill into the top of the boots, chilling the feet unless gaiters are used.

Boots should be warm and dry before skiing. Modern boots are great insulators. If the air held in the boots is cold, the boots will keep that air cold all day. When driving to the ski area, boots should be kept in the warm car (not in the trunk). They should be brought inside and dried carefully at night.

People who have previously had frostbite or who have circulation problems are subject to cold problems in ski boots. Boots with battery powered heating elements are a good investment for these individuals. Boot muffs add an effective layer of insulation to ski boots. They are highly recommended to anyone with the problem of cold feet. Chemical heat-generating packs can be installed in the boots to keep the foot warm. (Grabber Company makes an insole with a pocket for heat packs.)

9. How can you tell when the forward flex of a boot is too stiff?

A boot that is too stiff in forward flex can have some very negative consequences in skiing performance. The ankle is a very supple joint. Effective use of the ankle is of prime importance for good balance and smooth efficient skiing. When a boot is too stiff longitudinally, use of the ankle is stymied. The most obvious result is a poor hip position.

When the ankle is flexing adequately, the hips can be kept directly above the feet. When the ankles are not allowed to flex, the knees and the hips have to absorb all minor changes in skiing terrain. The hips end up flexing to a position behind the feet, and the skier appears to be squatting or sitting back. Tremendous stress is applied to the tops of the thighs. Softening the forward flex of the boot will dramatically improve the skier's ability to stand over the top of the boot.

Boots that are longitudinally too stiff apply severe leverage to the tips of the skis. This excess leverage will cause the ski tips to bite and hook. The skier will bounce and chatter through the turn. It will be very difficult for the skier to execute a smooth arc. The tails of the skis will have a tendency to "wash out" through the finish of the turn.

Boot testing and product development are typically done by accomplished, athletic male skiers. A boot that flexes well for the aggressive 170-pound male will be a monster for the 115-pound female. Even lower-level recreational boots are occasionally beefed up too much because of the product-testing process.

When the boot does not have a built-in flex adjustment, plastic components or post rivets, which restrict forward flexibility, can often be removed from a boot shell to greatly free forward flexibility.

10. How can you tell when a boot is the right size?

When a person initially puts on the correct size of a new ski boot, his response is usually that the boot is too small. It takes wearing the boot for a period of time and applying flexing pressures to the boot before the fit materials in the boot liner compress to the shape of the foot. Most boot liners enlarge dramatically with use. If the boot is bought with a roomy fit, after a minimum usage, the boot will feel too loose.

The boot-buying process should always start by measuring both feet with a scientific ski-boot sizing device. The size you wear in your sneakers is probably different from the size you will wear in a ski boot. With a properly sized front entry boot and occasionally in a rear entry boot, you will feel the end of the boot liner with the toes when the boot is first put on.

When the proper closure bales are closed, the buckles should not be more than a quarter of the way through their adjustments when the boot is snug. The boot needs to be worn at least five to ten minutes before the fit is evaluated. It is best to simulate skiing when trying on new boots. A Ski Legs exercise device, a ski simulator, a ski ramp or simply clamping the boots into a pair of rental bindings will allow edge-to-edge flexing movements that will speed the break-in process.

Boots are fit for skiing, not walking. Skiing uses different motions, muscles, and pressure dynamics than walking. A boot that fits well while walking probably will not fit well while skiing. Turn your mind off for the first five minutes while the fit materials adjust.

After the adjustment period, with the boot clamped down firmly, check the fit using the following criteria.

When you lean back, the toes should feel the front of the boot. When standing neutral (lower leg touching both the front and back of the boot cuff), you should just be aware of the front of the liner with a front entry boot, or you should be just off the front of the liner with a rear entry.

As you flex forward, the toes should be off the end of the boot, and the foot should remain securely in the bottom of the boot. If the heel lifts when the knee is flexed, you will probably get upward motion in the heel when skiing. You should not be able to slide the foot fore and aft in the boot. There should be no side-to-side motion in the boot.

The foot should feel firmly contained without any points or lines of pressure. If you have a somewhat unique foot, it may require some fit adjustments or some fit aids to achieve that feeling. A pronated foot will require a footbed or some insole wedging to reach that point.

A boot will not feel better on the hill. A customer should be content that the boots are snug, yet consistently smooth inside before the fitting process is complete.

PART III ALPINE BINDINGS

19 Indemnification Programs

Tremendous technical improvements in alpine ski bindings combined with more training and a higher level of service in retail ski shops have been responsible for a significant reduction in lower leg injuries in recent years. Today, all binding manufacturers conduct clinics for shop technicians and certify binding mechanics. With the sophisticated tools the mechanic has to work with, mounting bindings is no longer a job the average skier should attempt.

In addition to certification clinics, each manufacturer produces a detailed technical manual that provides the information the mechanic needs to work on specific binding models. By following the manufacturer's recommendations, the binding mechanic is also following the requirements of the manufacturer's indemnification program.

Since their introduction in 1975, indemnification programs developed by ski binding manufacturers have had a tremendous influence on the binding business worldwide. Although the first programs were developed to deal with the increasing liability problem being faced by retail ski shops (indemnification was also a new marketing strategy), the programs have brought about changes that have gone well beyond their original goals.

One positive, if indirect, result of indemnification has been a remarkable reduction in the types of injuries releasable bindings are designed to prevent.

Robert Johnson of the University of Vermont and Carl Ettlinger of Vermont Ski Safety began conducting a study of ski injuries at Glen Ellen, now Sugarbush North, in the early 1970s. At the end of the first fifteen years of the study, they were able to report to the International Symposium of Ski Trauma and Skiing Safety (ISSS) that their studies showed the overall injury rate among skiers had dropped 50 percent. Most of the improvement, they noted, has been in the reduction of lower leg injuries, particularly in the reduction of ankle sprains (down 86%) and tibia fractures (down 89%).

Statistically, it is impossible to determine how many injuries have been prevented only through the use of better bindings (better slope grooming, for example, has also played a role), but the connection is obvious. First, binding certification clinics held by the manufacturers to qualify binding mechanics have raised the skill level and knowledge level of the average shop binding technician. It is clear that the typical ski shop is selling a better product and providing better and more knowledgeable service today than it did in 1975.

Second, obsolescence (and the realities of a finite market) helped eliminate a dozen or more bindings of suspect performance capability. The adoption of ski boot DIN standards, for example, led to uniform sole shapes and helped make plate bindings less necessary. Besser, Moog, Americana, and similar bindings that were developed to compensate for different sole shapes and thicknesses were no longer technically valid.

Obsolescence, lagging technical development, and loss of marketing clout contributed to the disappearance of pioneering binding companies like Cubco and innovators like Spademan and Burt. The survivors, manufacturers who were investing heavily in research and development, have produced a line of more advanced, more sophisticated, and safer products. The elimination of technically inferior bindings and the training of skilled binding technicians has undoubtedly contributed to the reduction in the injuries noted by Ettlinger and Johnson.

What the indemnification programs also did was to define responsibility. The manufacturers were, in a sense, telling the ski shops that if the shop did a proper job of installation (following recommended procedures and certifying their binding mechanics), the manufacturer would protect the shop against suits brought by injured skiers.

"Indemnification programs are a contract between the manufacturer and the dealer," one binding supplier representative explained. "What we are saying to the shops is if they follow our recommended procedures, we will back them in court. It is not a bulletproof security blanket for the dealer. The retailer still has responsibility for following the procedures outlined in each manufacturer's technical manual."

When the skier picks up the equipment in the shop, the clerk and the customer validate the contract to confirm that the bindings were adjusted appropriately for the skier's height, weight, age, and skiing type. The clerk shows the skier that the release setting (commonly known as DIN) conforms to the ability level claimed by the customer.

Indemnification programs were inevitable. Without a list of rules and guidelines that the binding technician could follow (and a system to encourage that they were followed), there was no assurance that bindings would work as they were designed to work or that they would function to their maximum potential. Over the past few years, requirements have become tougher as the threat of litigation has increased. The industry, as a whole, has learned more about the function of boot and binding systems. The indemnification programs have, in effect, made the binding manufacturers and the retailer partners.

Tougher standards have not been without cost. One manufacturer estimates that about $6.00 in the wholesale price of every pair of bindings sold represents the amount the manufacturer must tack onto the price to cover the cost of existing and antici- pated lawsuits. It is a reflection of our litigious times and the attitude of our society.

For the skier, time-consuming in- spections and the testing of boot- binding systems have added cost at the retail level. But while service costs have increased, the actual cost of bindings since 1975 has dropped substantially when priced in inflation- adjusted dollars.

In the past dozen years, the cost- of-living index has more than doubled in the United States, but binding prices today for top-end models have increased, on average, only 40 to 50 percent. Mid-range models, which ac- tually cost about the same today as top-end models did in 1975, are tech- nically superior to the best bindings available at that time.

There are definitely valid reasons for encouraging skiers to update their bindings and justification for charging for improved and more extensive service. The combination of better service and better products is unques- tionably responsible for preventing thousands of lower leg injuries that may otherwise have occurred.

20 *Mounting Bindings*

Today, all binding manufacturers offer clinics and certification programs for shop personnel. Should mounting alpine bindings be a do-it-yourself project? The answer is no.

But the reality is that individual skiers, regardless of the hazards, do mount bindings on their own skis in the privacy of their own garages or basements and probably will continue to do so. There are a number of arguments that do-it-yourself binding mechanics use to justify mounting their own bindings. Most often mentioned are convenience, time, service, and cost. Taking every pair of skis that needs bindings mounted to a qualified binding technician is time-consuming, expensive, and not always convenient.

This is particularly true for working ski instructors or competitors who have reason to try different skis and switch bindings frequently. They argue, too, that a competent amateur may be capable of doing better work than an inadequately trained or careless shop employee. Possibly so. But a competent amateur without access

to the right jigs, drill bits, tapping tools, materials, and testing equipment will never match the work of a well-qualifed binding technician working in a shop.

Any skier with a few tools and basic technical skills can secure a pair of bindings to a pair of skis. That is not an overly complicated project. But doing a proper job requires more than a bench and a little enthusiasm. The home enthusiast does create problems for the binding manufacturers and distributors.

On one hand, manufacturers and distributors do everything possible to discourage skiers who want to mount their own bindings and they are reluctant to offer advice to the amateur. Most manufacturers no longer include paper templates in the boxes with the bindings they sell. On the other hand, while not encouraging the home mechanic, the binding manufacturers hope that if a skier does mount bindings at home, the work is done carefully and with some understanding of what is involved.

The situation is comparable to the scene in an old war movie where the captain of the submarine (thousands of miles from port and with no doctor on board) saves the life of the radio operator by removing his appendix using the cook's kitchen knives and a first-aid book as a guide. Most doctors will insist that an appendectomy is not a do-it-yourself project, but if circumstances make it unavoidable, it is important that the person doing the job has the best possible advice.

The most common mistake the home mechanic makes is failing to align the toe units correctly on the ski. Getting the screw holes in the proper place without a template is not as easy as it may seem. Without a template, it is difficult to keep the drill bit from traveling. Unless the toes are straight, it is difficult to obtain releases equally in both directions—a problem that would probably take a basic mechanical torque test to identify.

If the boot is misaligned on the ski, to get a release in one direction, the boot has to move past the center point. That increases the forces required before the boot can travel past center to go on to obtain a release. The release in the other direction is easier because the boot is already past the center point. The binding setting becomes, at best, a compromise.

The consumer, without access to the current adjustment tables supplied by the manufacturer and the same technical information available to the shop technician, may not know what size holes to drill, the hole depths, screw sizes, or tapping instructions or understand that recommendations from individual ski manufacturers may differ. Testing, experience, and research have also led to changes in the adjustment tables that may

occur annually.

It is possible to delaminate or ruin the top skin of an expensive pair of skis, dimple or puncture the base, or have screws pull out at an inopportune moment. These are problems that are not covered by either ski or binding warranties. Even if the home mechanic is capable of securing the binding to the ski correctly, there is no way of testing to make sure the boots and bindings are compatible and that the system is working properly. This requires a mechanical testing device.

To conform to recommended ASTM standards (and to meet requirements for indemnification programs), boot and binding combinations must be tested using a mechanical testing device. It is impossible for the home mechanic to test boot and binding systems without a basic testing device.

With all of the reasons against doing binding installation at home, are there any exceptions?

Doing your own bindings is not worth it if the main reason is to save money. But if there is not a local shop available or no shop with a technician certified to mount the brand of bindings you own, and if you feel you are really capable of doing the work, make certain you have the right tools and the right technical information.

Read the available directions carefully. Find out what the ski manufacturer recommends for mounting bindings on the particular ski model you are working with. Skis with metal tops or skis with phenolic mounting plates, for example, usually require tapping.

If the toe is secured by three screws, locate the exact center of the ski for the location of the front screw.

Note, too, that the sides of the skis are not parallel. So a square placed along one side of the ski will not give you a correct line across the ski for placement of the rear screws.

Another common problem in working without a template is placing the heel unit the right distance from the toe. The heel must be located on the correct position on the track so the boot is positioned to allow enough elasticity to enable the system to function properly.

The manufacturers understand why a skier who likes to work with tools and who has the necessary technical skills might prefer mounting his or her own bindings. If you do mount your own bindings, when you are finished, find a shop either near where you live or at an area where you ski and have the system inspected and tested. If you have followed all the instructions and worked carefully, the chances are that the system will pass. It does not pay to take a chance.

21 *Standards*

ASTM

ASTM (American Society for Testing and Materials) procedures for mounting and testing ski boot and binding combinations in retail ski shops and rental shops have become the acceptable standard of care in the United States. Compliance with the ASTM standards is voluntary. One of the objectives when the process of developing industry standards began was to develop voluntary procedures for the ski industry. The alternative was to risk having less desirable standards imposed on the industry by federal regulations.

Voluntary as ASTM standards may be, however, any shop not adopting the recommended standards would have difficulty defending itself in litigation. These procedures are required by all ski binding manufacturers as a key part of their indemnification programs. The recommendations that have been debated and accepted as prudent shop practices have evolved as "a higher standard of care." They have become, in effect, de facto standards recognized by the binding manufacturers and the insurance industry.

Although it is not necessary to know the history of the ASTM process to meet ASTM standards, the history includes a good deal of useful background information that demonstrates how the process has encouraged the industry to make skiing a safer sport.

Current ASTM standards involve Retail Shop Practices, Rental Shop Practices, and Incomplete Systems. The Incomplete Systems was responsible for developing standards for rental and demonstration equipment when the skier contributes one or more of the components that make up the release system. An example is when skiers provide their own boots when renting skis. The Shop Practices subcommittee includes ski equipment manufacturers, retail and rental ski shop operators, insurance companies, representatives from SIA and NSAA, and individuals who are experts in related fields such as engineering and sports medicine.

Since the drafting of ASTM ski standards began in 1971, individually proposed standards have been revised and rewritten as experience, research, and the introduction of new products, technology, and techniques have dictated. The standards approved at the society level in 1989 will be reviewed automatically every five years and continue to be revised and rewritten based on experience, research, and changes in technology.

Testing

The purpose of testing is to determine how well a boot and binding work together, not as a test of individual components. It is possible that testing will catch a manufacturing defect in a toe or heel unit if a defective unit has slipped through at the source. But no manufacturer has control over how the bindings are handled and installed once they have been shipped from the factory.

DIN manufacturing standards followed by the binding manufacturers in Europe, where almost all alpine bindings distributed in the United States are manufactured, apply to bindings and are only indirectly related to how the binding functions as an individual component of a system that involves multiple parts.

The successful test of a new system guarantees that the heel and toe have been mounted correctly and that, at the time the equipment is carried out of the shop, the boots being used by the skier are compatible and function properly with the bindings—that the system works as the designers intended, as well as current technology allows. The guarantee is not that the skier will not or cannot be injured but that based on current technology, the essential, prudent steps have been taken to reduce the probability of injury.

An ASTM task force conducted tests in 1988 which confirmed the fact that combinations made up of new components fall outside even 20 percent tolerances approximately 23 percent of the time. As there is an almost limitless number of boot and binding combinations, random testing of new components, as opposed to testing all new boot and binding combinations, is considered illogical. Drafted ASTM standards have already had an influence on retail and rental shop practices before they were finally approved, so there was less urgency by the ASTM committee to produce a final set of standards.

Looking ahead, there are several developments likely to influence how bindings are tested and serviced in the future. The testing of new systems is required as there is currently no logical way the manufacturer can guarantee performance when the binding is installed as one part of a boot/binding system. Even strict manufacturing standards are not guarantees of compatibility. The recommended settings on the charts provided to the retail shops by the manufacturers will also be modified as additional data is collected on performance characteristics and as technical product changes are made.

Retesting

There will be an emphasis on the retesting of previously tested systems. The ASTM standards, as written, concern testing of systems in the store. Binding wear, boot wear, corrosion, general neglect, or attempts by the skier to readjust a system can create failures in performance. Neither the retailer nor the binding manufacturer can guarantee the performance of a system over an indefinite period of time.

An emphasis on maintenance and retesting will shift some responsibility for performance to the individual skier who may be held responsible for periodic retesting. Frequent retesting helps assure performance. The buyer of a new car, for example, may invalidate a warranty by not following the manufacturers' service recommendations.

Another goal is for the acceptance of minimum boot and binding performance standards internationally. Today, binding manufacturers who distribute their products internationally in less litigation-conscious countries indemnify retailers and require performance testing only in the United States. For all the expense and inconvenience, the higher standard of care enjoyed by U.S. skiers has produced an injury rate below that of any other alpine nation.

Retailers

Improving the level of safety is a logical concern of everyone involved in skiing, both for humanitarian reasons and for economic reasons: an injured skier does not ski. The retailers, the binding manufacturers, and the volunteer members of the ASTM committees have made important contributions to the improvement of the sport. Despite the inconvenience, time, and expense, any retailer with high standards must find satisfaction in being able to send a customer out the door with equipment that he knows is in the best possible condition—a job well done.

The Role of the United States

The ASTM is unique throughout the world because of its rules on developing consensus and its strict by-laws regarding balloting procedures and the rights of minority opinions. The process has made the United States the leader in improved safety standards. The rest of the skiing world has been primarily concerned with manufacturing a product and being able to export it without restrictions and selling it within their own borders. The process of providing a product that their experts believe is safe has taken a very simplistic and often discriminatory role in restricting innovation and change.

Some ASTM standards have become international standards and are today practiced throughout the world. The voluntary standard of care by ski shops in the United States involves procedures that are not enjoyed or even available in most other countries of the world.

Resisting Standards

Although the standards would appear to work to the advantage of both the skiing public and the retail shops, resistance has come on several different levels. The first level is the dealer reaction to being told what to do. This is often conditioned by past misunderstandings of the standards process, its goals, and who is involved.

The fear of most retailers who have resisted the adoption of standards is that responsibility for performance is being shifted from the manufacturer to the retailer and that, eventually, the manufacturers will drop their indemnification programs. Ultimately, in any lawsuit, the court determines where liability lies. The manufacturer has an interest in retaining indemnification programs because they give the manufacturer some control over how the product is used.

The second area of concern that people have is that their product or service will be maligned or discriminated against or in some way be made less profitable by the implementation of the standards. At this level, it is easier to discuss or debate the issues.

The ASTM recommendations at the retail level add about three to five minutes to the old procedures. If properly integrated, it can be almost transparent in terms of the management of the ski shop. The typical numbers are for shops that have multiple mechanics and have a well-laid-out service center where thay can process five systems per mechanic per hour.

Following ASTM testing procedures, they are processing four systems per mechanic per hour. If ski tuning and other services, like putting a protective ski care coating on top of the skis are added, a mechanic still is able to put out three systems per hour.

When there is a minor increase in the time it takes to put the whole system out the door, it does not seem to be an onerous procedure, something that shops should be concerned about in terms of the bottom-line cost. It is also something that should be looked on as an opportunity. That is because most of the service work is not on totally new systems but on systems that include used equipment.

The complete inspection of the system as it is assembled from partly new and partly used equipment is something that the customer should be expected to pay for. In fact, it should be a service the customer should seek out. It is an opportunity for the shop to provide a valuable, necessary service to the customer and to be able to charge a reasonable fee.

The ski binding distributors probably deserve most of the credit for having moved the ASTM program forward. But the manufacturers are caught in somewhat of a bind. In the United States, the concern is with the performance of the entire system. There are incompatibilities between the design standards of the components and the performance standards that are being discovered independently in this country. The manufacturers would like to see one comprehensive world standard.

Their job is not made easier by having different national standards. The United States is a user country, not a producer country. Efforts in the United States are always going to be more effective in developing use standards—the performance standards for the final system—than individual product design standards.

DIN

Most new ski boots on the market today conform to specifications established by the West German standards organization, Deutsche Industrie Normen (DIN). The DIN standard establishes the scale for release values used for ski binding adjustments and sets standards for boot sole dimensions—shape and thickness.

While most boots do conform to DIN specifications, what concerns boot and binding manufacturers are the exceptions—boots that do not conform to DIN; boots that do conform but are not identified as DIN; and boots that are stamped DIN but do not necessarily conform. The initials, ISO, are often used interchangeably with DIN.

Although DIN standards are not directly related to the new ASTM standards for shop practices, skiers and shop personnel have come to rely on the DIN binding scale and DIN-established boot dimensions as indicators that the products they buy or work with will work together and test out as compatible. There are several things to consider when working with these products. First, just because a boot has DIN stamped on it does not mean it is going to be compatible with every ski binding. What matters is whether it is compatible with the specific binding the boot is being used with. Second, when a manufacturer stamps DIN on the sole of the boot, the manufacturer is saying the boot meets DIN specifications. If you have a boot that also has the stamp IAS or TUF, for example, that means that the boot has been tested in an independent laboratory and meets DIN standards. There is a difference. If you add the logo of a laboratory that certifies the boot meets the standards, it means that the product you have in your hands has been approved.

Another problem is a boot that met DIN specifications when it was new but because of wear or boot damage may no longer meet DIN specifications. There are also boots that are not stamped DIN but function properly when tested in a boot and binding system. There is the problem that a mold may meet the standards and the boot may meet the dimensional standards, but the boot may be made of a material that is too soft.

All these considerations are trivial compared to the primary issue, which is whether or not a specific boot is compatible with a specific binding. Shop personnel should not rely too much on the initials stamped on the boot sole. When the DIN standard was established, it essentially recognized a boot sole shape that already existed. What counts is how the final system performs—how the indvidual components work together. There is a general recognized set of objective tests that can be made on the equipment.

ASTM has developed performance standards that emphasize the entire system. A ski boot and binding system only exists for the first time in the hands of the binding mechanic. DIN specifications are for components only.

In the United States, the concentration is on performance standards for the end product, while in Europe the concentration is on design standards for the components. The primary difference in the standards established in Germany and the testing standards developed through ASTM is in the end goal.

In the United States, we are a user country, not a producer country. Instead of competing with DIN to come up with design standards, we have developed performance standards. Our standards are voluntary and would not have the same impact that DIN has. Germany is the only country in the world in which DIN standards are actually law.

A design standard cannot guarantee compatibility. If you were to guarantee shape under load, you would have to define stiffness and hardness of the boot sole as well as shape. Those two terms have never been defined in a standard. What is important is what shape the boot is going to have once the surfaces are loaded.

Performance problems are exaggerated if the boot material is soft. What you really care about is something called rolling friction. When the surface of the boot sole is forced over another surface, like a roller in a binding, additional work is being expended just to get the boot out of the binding because the boot material is not hard enough. Standards for coefficient of friction are included in the ASTM standards, but there are no definitions for hardness.

To make a design standard so tight that it could guarantee compatibility would take too much discretion away from boot manufacturers. Part of the problem is simply that bindings can be made to uniform sizes, but feet cannot, so boots cannot.

Considering the liability potential, why would a boot manufacturer produce a boot and put a DIN stamp on it if the boot did not meet DIN specifications? The manufacturer may not know it does not meet DIN specifications. As a practical matter, not every product has to meet the DIN standard. Only a certain number of production samples have to pass.

In establishing standards, it is recognized that not every boot will fall within the same exact tolerances. In normal production, a certain number of boots can fall outside of the tolerances while the specifications remain valid. Again, what really counts is how an individual boot works with a specific binding. The performance of the system as it is put together in the retail shop is the primary concern.

22 *Testing Boot-Binding Systems*

Every ski shop in the United States which rents, sells, or services alpine equipment should already own at least one device capable of measuring the force or torque required to release a boot from a binding. Testing of boot-binding systems is required by all alpine binding manufacturers as a condition of current indemnification agreements.

Since the commercial demise of such systems as the Kwik Chek, Hydrocheck, Lipe, and Look devices, the market for such machines has been dominated by the Vermont Calibrator, the hand-held, torque measuring device designed by Carl Ettlinger and distributed through his company, Vermont Ski Safety Equipment, and also by The Tool Company of New Hampshire.

Recently, European-made machines have appeared in the United States. All the European-manufactured testing devices were produced originally to be used in Europe and designed to meet European testing standards. In Europe, the testing involves a measurement of force, while the U.S. system uses torque. Con-sequently, the European-built testing machines must be modified to be usable in the United States. It is possible that a system will evolve soon to standardize testing internationally to resolve this problem. As indemnification programs, as well as prudent shop practices, make the owning of a testing device all but mandatory, the market for these devices in the United States is large.

The technology is changing rapidly. New machines are being introduced and existing testing machines are being modified as testing parameters are changed. Any list of testing devices will be outdated quickly. The basic functions of the testing devices that meet testing requirements will not change, but the retail shop owner interested in information on specific machines can only turn to the manufacturer for current information.

Force Testing versus Torque Testing

The ASTM standards for ski shop testing of boot-binding systems make no distinction between the use of force and torque measuring devices. Either type of device is acceptable to binding manufacturers who indemnify shops for working on their products. So why should someone who is shopping for a test device care if it measures force or torque?

Because the accuracy of force measuring devices depends on an assumption, made by either the operator or the machine, as to what part of the boot is really operating as a lever to release the binding. Because of the design differences among bindings, one model may use more, or less, of the total boot sole length as its effective lever arm than another. If the operator or test device manufacturer misjudges the lever arm, the torque value derived from the machine's force measurement will be inaccurate. A machine that measures torque directly helps reduce the error in selecting the appropriate release adjustment for the skier—which is the whole point of testing.

This is not to say that force measurements, whether toe or heel, will not work properly, as long as the operator and/or machine correctly predicts the length of the boot sole's true lever arm. If the Calibrator is more sensitive to the operator influence at the heel, the electromechanical devices are more likely to be design sensitive, with an inherent bias for those bindings with a lever arm length closest to the machine's estimate.

As one might expect, every supplier of a test machine believes theirs is the fastest. Estimates range from 3 minutes a pair (ours) to 12 minutes (theirs) to run through all the tests. Of course, speed depends on what procedures are being counted as part of

the testing and what one considers a complete test to be. Tests run by retail shop personnel have not found significant differences in the time required to test bindings using a variety of testing devices. Inexperienced operators of different heights obtained different results when using the Calibrator, but people make the mistakes, not the machines. None of the machines are foolproof.

If one distills all the various reports, it appears that an experienced operator can learn to inspect a pair of bindings in about five minutes, no matter what machine he or she uses. Any troubleshooting, or extensive clean versus lubricated testing, adds time to this base figure.

Some advocates of computerized machines believe that it would be faster if they were not required to obtain three releases in each direction tested. But three measured releases, or two identical releases, are a requirement imposed by the binding manufacturers to ensure a representative result that can only be waived by the binding manufacturer.

While speed is a consideration, accuracy is not. Any of the current devices can be abused. The best guarantee of accuracy is a thorough understanding of how the test device works. All of them require some degree of training. The higher costs of the automatic, electric machines are not a guarantee of greater reliability but are perhaps justified by an edge in marketing. Electronic devices look more high-tech and printed results seem somehow more conclusive.

This suggests that if you are going to aggressively market your testing program and make equipment testing a front-room operation at least part of the year, the electronic devices represent an interesting alternative to the less expensive, more rustic looking, Vermont Calibrator. And the electronic devices may be better at dousing fires sparked by obsolescence and potential shop liability. Ultimately, the choice of test devices will be less important than learning the proper application of whatever device is used.

23 The Chord-Length System

The job of determining the binding location on a new pair of skis has been made simpler in recent years. Most ski manufacturers mark the center of the ski with a line on the top of the ski or on the side wall. Boot manufacturers put a midsole mark on the side of the boot sole. If you get the two marks together and the ball of the foot is over the center of the running surface of the ski, you are ready to begin boring holes. Right? Not necessarily.

It is a simple system that is satisfactory in most cases, but not everyone believes it is the ideal system. Most binding technicians go along with the system and use the mid-sole mark. This is the one most people are familiar with. But there are still believers in the chord-length system used by many craftsmen which locates the toe of the boot on the ski as the guide to determining binding placement.

One of the problems in using the toe mark instead of the mid-sole mark is that efforts to teach the chord-length system proved too difficult. It is easier to use the center mark system.

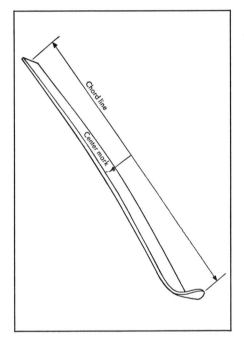

The chord length is the straight-line distance from the tip of the ski to the tail. Occasionally, factory technicians are asked if the measurement is from the front of the tip or from the back of the tip. It is from the back of the tip, but this is not important. It only makes a millimeter or two difference. It only takes a few seconds for technicians working with bindings to

108

measure the chord length. The binding placement system using the boot toe requires measuring the chord length of the ski, then dividing that length in half to determine the location of the toe of the boot. The recommended placement is one centimeter ahead of the center mark, which works best for most skiers, with some exceptions.

Using the center chord mark for locating the boot toe is the system used by many racing service technicians mounting bindings on racing or high performance skis. The most common placement is one centimeter ahead of the mid-chord mark for slalom skis, on the mid-chord mark for giant slalom skis, and one centimeter behind the mid-chord mark for downhill skis.

There should be little difference in binding location using either the mid-chord length or the mid-sole boot mark for skiers with average-size boots—eight, nine, or ten. The differences begin to appear with skiers with small feet, including many women skiers. If you use the mid-sole boot system, skiers with small boot sizes find the toe of the boot beginning to move to the rear away from where it would be using the mid-chord length system.

Using the chord-length method also eliminates the possibility that the mid-sole line or a boot toe line has been silk screened onto the ski in the wrong place. Mistakes are made if the worker in the factory doing the silk screening lets the jig slip a little bit or forgets to move the jog when changing from one model length to another.

Advocates of the chord-length system believe it is a good idea for the shop technician to measure the ski and make sure that the line is in the real world.

PART IV CROSS-COUNTRY AND TELEMARK SKIS

24 *Tuning*

Cross-country racers, serious track skiers, and telemarkers have long known that a well-tuned ski provides better performance and adds significantly to the life of the ski. Waxless and waxable skis are the two basic types of cross-country skis on the market today. Waxless skis with "fish scales" or similar patterns cut into the polyethylene base require the least care, but they still need waxing and occasional base or edge repair. They perform better if the base is kept clean. The application of a wipe-on liquid or paste wax helps clean the base, but wipe-on wax will not last long. Ironed-on wax is far superior but requires care in application. Good results also can be obtained by rubbing glide wax on the tips and tails and then corking.

Waxable skis require a more sophisticated approach to get the best results. There are important factors in tuning waxable cross-country skis which differ from tuning alpine skis with their extruded polyethylene or sintered bases. While cross-country skis are sometimes described as "skinny" downhill skis, there are major differences between the two that require specific techniques and tools to achieve optimum performance and to protect them from damage.

Traditional telemark skis were long, laminated wood boards with pine tar bases and hard, wood composite edges. Ski tuning materials consisted of a sanding block and a metal scraper, with a flaming torch nearby and the strong smell of pine tar in the air.

Times have changed. The best Nordic downhill skis today are simply skinny alpine skis with offset steel edges, P-tex bases, and vibration-dampening construction. For skiers taking up telemarking or skiers already involved in the sport, telemark tuning involves few mysteries. The steps are similar to those required to tune a pair of alpine skis. Because telemark skis can be sensitive and a bit edge catchy, proper tuning is at least as important as tuning traditional alpine skis.

Cleaning

A clean base is essential when tuning. Dirt and grime in the snow and pollutants in the air work their way into ski bases, increasing the ski's drag and lessening its ability to absorb wax. To achieve optimal performance and to extend the life of the ski, bases should be cleaned frequently.

Cleaning can be done in several ways. One is to apply a wax remover with a rag, flooding the base and wiping it clean. Another method is to iron on a soft wax with a low melting point and wipe it off while still molten. Do this several times. The heat expands the microstructure of the polyethylene, and the hot wax floats out particles of dust and dirt. Apply enough wax so that the iron can move freely back and forth. Too little wax can let the iron touch the base directly, damaging it.

Factory-fresh skis can have a hard, impermeable surface finish as a result of the manufacturing process itself. Some companies are shaving off a layer of base as the last step in the manufacturing process to create a clean base.

There are different opinions on how to achieve a clean base on new skis. Some technicians shy away from belt sanding and prefer to use a metal scraper. Many race technicians use an inexpensive metal scraper to shave the base. These scrapers are stamped out of sheet steel, creating a burred edge, which helps peel off base material. One scraper can be used effectively on only two or three pairs of skis. After scraping, follow up with several passes of a Fibertex pad, then more scraping. This process is not recommended for the recreational skier.

Others use a belt sander with an old, worn belt. Since Nordic skis only have five-eighths the mass of alpine skis and no steel edges, belt sanders or grinders have a much greater impact on the skis. Scratches put into a sintered base with a grinder will be very difficult to remove. And with the high heat generated by a grinder or belt sander, the possibility exists for delaminating the ski.

High-performance Nordic skis are often finished with a built-in base structure designed for optimum performance on a wide range of snow conditions. Keep base sanding and preparation to a minimum to retain this built-in structure for as long as possible.

Procedures

The basic process of tuning waxable cross-country skis mirrors the tuning of downhill skis. A well-equipped ski shop will need few if any special tools. Two exceptions are a rilling tool for base structuring and a cross-country ski vise. The proper vise is more important in working with cross-country skis than with alpine skis because Nordic skis are very flexible and require more support. The best is a full-length profile vise that provides support the length of the ski. If alpine ski vises are used, the vises must be placed close together with additional support for the tips and tails.

Base Preparation

Friction is the enemy of fast skiing. While there is nothing you can do to change snow conditions created by temperature, humidity, and track preparation, you can tune the ski. Stiffness, length and width, base material, base surface treatment, and waxing are the subfactors in the ski's friction equation. Of these factors, the most easily controlled are base surface and waxing.

With waxable skis, always check the base for flatness first using a true bar. The base should be flat from side to side as well as from tip to tail. Hold the ski up to a light source and move the true bar down the full length of the ski, looking for daylight between the ski base and the bar. A black-colored true bar works best as it is more glare-free. Light shining under the bar will show where the P-tex base or the metal edges are low. High bases should be scraped or ground down. Although ski manufacturers are delivering well-tuned skis fresh from the factory, some may have convex or concave bases as the result of the shrinking and expanding of base materials. Many telemark skis come excessively base-high from the factory. This gives the ski bottom a convex shape. Base-high skis are "squirrely" and unstable.

Skis with high bases are easier to ski than those with low or concave bases. Such bases are called "railed," and skis with railed bases are slow to turn and hook easily when skied across the fall line.

Hand-sanding with a sanding block is the most common method for flattening bases. Begin with 80- or 100-weight paper and move up to 150- or 180-weight paper, scraping between changes in paper weight. If the base is excessively high, it is best to have them stone ground or scrape them flat with a metal scraper.

Once the base is flat, check for burrs, gouges, and nicks. Burrs can be buffed off with Fibertex or re-moved with a steel scraper. However, take care with a scraper as it can easily damage the base you worked so hard to flatten.

Base gouges and nicks can be repaired using the same techniques used on downhill skis. Clean the damaged area and, if the area is small or shallow, fill with a P-tex candle. If the damage is excessive, cut away the damaged area and replace it with a patch of the same base material glued with epoxy. Scrape the excess away using a Sur-form tool or scraper, then sand smooth.

Skis with high or railed edges should be flat filed using a 10-inch mill bastard file. Some prefer an auto body file or Pansar, but with these aggressive tools you must know exactly when to stop. Be careful not to bend the file when you grip it. Keep it flat. Place the file on the ski at an angle so that its teeth will cut. You will get the feel of the best angle according to the design of the file. You can push or pull the file, whichever is more comfortable, but the file's tang should always point away from the cutting direction.

File with long, smooth strokes. Clean the file often with the brush side of a card file. The metal side dulls a file and is best saved for hard-to-remove wax residue and plastic filings. Keep the base free of filings with a rag or brush. File the edges until they are flush with the base, checking the ski frequently with a true bar.

Dulling Edges

Next turn your attention to the ski edges. Slight dulling of the base edge on cross-country skis helps make them faster. For skating skis, most like to keep the 90-degree base edge sharp. If there are nicks, sand them out using 180-weight paper. Some technicians suggest dulling the tips back a bit farther than with downhill skis, because the ski is typically longer than a downhill ski.

Repairing gouges that penetrate the top skin or side walls can be a serious problem. Most side wall damage occurs when the skis are transported in a ski bag. The bindings from one pair are often forced into the side walls of another, damaging them. If the ski core is of foam or honeycomb construction, deep gouges can allow water to penetrate into the core. The water may cause the ski interior to expand and crack, weakening or delaminating the ski.

If the ski has a wood core (generally found in skating skis), or the nick just mars the surface, it should be filled with a marine epoxy paint, preferably one that requires 24 hours to dry. This also works well for repairing ski tails that have been jammed into the snow and delaminated. Use tape around the damaged area to serve as a dam, then apply the repair material, Sur-form or file away the excess, and sand smooth.

Structuring

Tuning cross-country skis for racing should also include base structuring. Skis most often glide on a thin film of water created by the heat of friction. If a ski base is perfectly smooth, the ski and the water layer act like two panes of wet glass stuck together, which hinders smooth gliding and easy turning. Structuring creates a texture in the ski's base to allow water film to dissipate.

In general the following rules apply. As speed increases, the need for structuring increases. The warmer the temperature and wetter the snow, the coarser the structure must be.

There are several ways to apply structure. Many high-performance skis come with structure applied by stone grinding at the factory. Stone grinders can be used to renew or apply different structure.

Some technicians say that stone-ground structures on Nordic skis are less effective than on downhill skis. This is due to higher pressures, narrower skis, and slower speeds associated with cross-country skiing. Using a stone grinder for cross-country structuring requires extreme care to avoid overheating the base and removing too much base material.

Belt sanders can also be used for structuring, but sanders leave behind microfibers. Belt sanding should be followed by buffing with a Fibertex pad or light scraping with a steel scraper.

The most common method of structuring is by hand. Snow conditions can change from hour to hour, and races are often held far from shop facilities. Hand structuring—on-site—provides the greatest flexibility and precision. Structure can be applied by hand in several ways, including use of a rilling tool, a metal brush, or sanding. Rilling tools, such as Swix's Structure Bar (T-180) or Super Riller (T-401), contain rows of small cutting teeth that are pressed into the base.

Push the riller tip to tail. Follow up by using Scotch-brite or Fibertex pads before waxing. Many technicians prefer to structure before waxing, but a skier can take off too much wax by rilling, which, in effect, is like using a metal scraper.

You can use a coarse steel wire brush to create structure. The brush should be pushed and pulled along the length of the ski, followed by a final pass from tip to tail.

Sandpaper can also be used. Generally use 100-weight paper. Work with a sanding block from tip to tail, followed by Fibertex. If it is extremely cold or there is new, dry snow, use a 150- to 180-weight paper, followed by steel scraping.

Waxing

The final step is waxing the prepared base. In addition to waxing for skiing, skis should be waxed for storage or transport using a soft, low-temperature wax. This protects skis from oxidation and from binding nicks when they are placed in ski bags.

Because Nordic skis are lighter and more fragile than their alpine cousins, you must be careful not to overheat the base when ironing on wax. Drip wax onto the base in two parallel lines. Press the selected wax bar onto the iron and dribble it along the base. Take the iron and pass it over the melted wax, evenly distributing it on the base.

Keep the iron moving constantly or you may cause the base to bubble or peel. Such damage is not covered by a manufacturers' warranty. Traditional waxes require minimal heat, but the new synthetic hydrocarbon waxes require higher heat and should be applied with care.

If the ski is being prepared for traditional stride skiing, roughen up the "kick zone" and apply your climbing wax or klister. Kick wax is often applied in layers because it is easier to cork. For abrasive conditions, use 100-grit paper to roughen the kick zone followed with a Scotch-brite or Fibertex pad.

Results from tuning cross-country skis are most apparent on a groomed track. Good tuning also improves performance for backcountry skiing, but deep snow and radical snow conditions make the benefits less noticeable. However, whether you ski a groomed track or rough backcountry, extra care in tuning will assure a longer-lasting ski.

Edge Beveling

Alpine skiers are very familiar with edge beveling. It is as important, if not more important, for telemark skis. Beveling improves turn initiation. It also reduces the "catchy" feeling so aggravating in three-pin skis and so conducive to outside edge falls.

Beveling minimizes that too-sharp sensation in soft and crusty snow and on steep slopes. And, with beveled edges, you can ski those skinny boards with more angulation rather than using the upright Nordic stance.

Telemark skis can be stone ground and edge beveled to the skier's specific instructions. Many telemark skiers prefer about a one degree of bevel. This is not a lot. Some alpine skiers use up to three degrees.

Many gate racers bevel the tips and tails more than the center of the ski. You can experiment with different degrees of bevel, but if you bevel telemark skis too much, they will have to be tipped so far over to engage the edge that their wide Nordic bindings can catch in the snow.

There is no mystery to edge beveling. If you do not have the heavy machinery to do it, you have some very simple options. The most foolproof and accurate method for at-home use is a quality hand beveler. If you are buying a hand-beveling tool, be sure it can bevel the base edge; many can bevel only the side edge. If your beveling tool is adjustable, the recommended setting is one degree for beveling the bottom edge of a telemark ski. Bevel the side edge one degree also. This keeps the edge profile close to 90 degrees, assuring the best bite. Follow the instructions included with your tool for both procedures.

To bevel with a file and duct tape, carefully wrap the end of your 10-inch or 12-inch file with two wraps of tape. Rub the tape flat. Place the file on the ski with the tape over one edge and the file over the other edge. The tape will lift one side of the file so that it tunes the opposite side with a slight bevel.

File with long, smooth strokes—as if you were flat filing. You can monitor your edge bevel by the new metal exposed as you file. Or if you are not sure of yourself, use a side-filing trick—color the edge with a Magic Marker before filing. Then file until the edge is beveled its full width and all the ink is gone. Turn the file around and repeat the process on the other edge.

Side Filing

The best telemark skis have offset edges just like alpine skis. You can side file with an offset edge to restore them to 90 degrees after base edge beveling and to remove nicks and burrs. To start, put your skis firmly in a vise. If the ski has any edge damage, stone its edges first to smooth any burrs and minimize the wear on your file. If the ski has an offset edge, you can hold the file in the palm of your hand and run it in smooth, long strokes. Be sure to keep the file flat against the edge and side wall.

If the side wall is not offset, hold the file in both hands at an angle to the edge as though you were flat filing. In this case, you will need to keep the thumbs pressed right over the edge to keep from bending the file. It is important to file evenly, perpendicular to the ski base.

If new metal is exposed evenly along the full width of the edge, you are doing fine. Use the Magic Marker trick. Color the side edge with the marker and then evenly file off the ink.

After sharpening the edges, you should remove any burrs created by the file and then dull the edges back from the tips and the tails. A too-sharp burr can hang up a ski in a turn, making it act like it was railed.

A burr stick, a rubberlike stone, works well. It has the right amount of abrasive material and removes burrs without dulling the edges. Run it along the edge from tip to tail. If you do not have a burr stick, lightly run a fine whetstone or emery paper the full length of the edge at a 45-degree angle to the base. Use the burr stick or stone to then dull the edges back 15 centimeters from the contact point on each ski's tip and tail. If you are skiing on packed slopes, carry a small stone or emery paper.

Once your skis have been properly tuned, you will never want to go back to an untuned ski—whether telemark, cross-country, or alpine. To keep them at their best, occasionally touch them up with a stone or do a light side filing. Keep them sharp, especially underfoot.

25 Base Structuring for Cross-Country Skis

Structuring the base on cross-country skis is perhaps easier than determining which of the various structuring techniques will best suit individual needs and snow conditions. Once you have determined which of the techniques is best for the time and place, the actual work involved is relatively easy.

New skis often have an uneven or slightly wavy base. For racing skis, these oscillation spots, left from the factory grinding process, can be detrimental to speed. To eliminate the high and low spots along the base, sand from tip to tail with number 100 grit racing paper. Occasionally remove the ski from the vise and sight along the base to check for any spots that have become highlighted by the sanding.

Continue sanding until all high spots have been removed and the base has an even sanding pattern. This can take from just a few minutes to as long as half an hour for each ski depending on the condition of the base and the base material. Several sandpaper changes might also be required.

Once new skis are properly finished, this process does not need to be repeated. A variety of techniques have been developed to follow up this initial treatment for new skis. The treatments outlined here are for competition skis but can be adapted to any ski. The specific steps to follow are determined by snow conditions and the type of skiing the skis will be used for.

The science of friction predicts that two smooth, polished surfaces will slide poorly on each other. If two sheets of glass are placed together with a film of water between them, it is very difficult to slide them apart. But when one or both surfaces are textured, grooved, or "rilled," there is a release of surface tension and the friction is reduced.

Skis sliding over snow react in a similar way, especially when the snow is slushy or saturated with water. Glide is improved on all types of snow when the base of the skis has been rilled, most notably when the air temperature is above freezing and there is free water present in the snow. In cold temperatures, rilled bases reduce the amount of surface contact between the base and snow. At above freezing temperatures, where free water exists, the rilled base allows water release. At temperatures between the two extremes, the rilled base may offer a combination of the two—less surface contact and less surface tension from the microscopic water vapor or layer. Rilling also offers stability by way of the small longitudinal grooves in the base.

Use of the rilling tool should be limited to skis that are going to be used on trails prepared by modern trail preparation machinery. The natural state of snow is greatly altered by trail setting equipment. The milling, molding, and compaction of the snow leads to snow crystals that are blunter and more rounded, breaking down the classic sharp-pointed crystals. If the snow is allowed to remain in its natural state, or if there is fresh snow falling during a race, rilled bases do not work well.

Several equipment and tool suppliers sell riller bars. Most are brass, a softer metal than steel, and are produced to use on alpine skis. Brass can be used without damaging steel edges. Riller bars are available with fine and course teeth, usually 0.5 mm or 0.75 mm. As an alternative to a riller bar, some ski tuners have tried to use the narrow edge of a file with less than satisfactory results.

Swix has a rilling tool, the T-401 Riller, with three different cutter blades. The Swix riller tool has spring loaded guides on the sides. It slides over the tip of the ski and is pushed down the ski to make parallel grooves.

The standard cutting bar, 0.75 mm, is for general use on most snow and

Rilling Tools

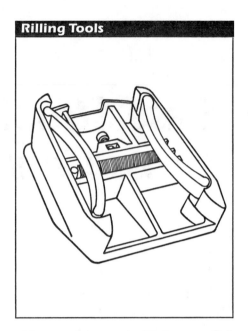

old snow down to −10 degrees Celsius or −14 degrees Fahrenheit. The coarse cutting bar, 1.0 mm, is for wet saturated snow and the fine 0.5 mm bar is for compacted snow or snow prepared with machinery at −10 degrees Celsius or colder.

Rilling Methods

The skis should be clean prior to rilling since dirt and wax will dull and clog the cutting teeth. Using firm, even pressure, push the riller bar or T-401 Riller tool from tip to tail. If you use the riller tool, face the arrow on the riller in the direction of tip to tail. For skating skis, do the entire length. For traditional skiing, do the glide zones. After rilling, the base should be buffed with Fibertex to reduce any sharp edges on the rills and to eliminate any microscopic polyethylene burrs.

Waxing

Iron glide wax on in the usual manner. When the wax has cooled and hardened to room temperature, scrape off the excess wax with a plastic scraper. Use light strokes when scraping since a sharp scraper can cut away the rills. After scraping, it is important to brush the remaining wax out of the rills with a nylon brush with fine, stiff bristles. Repeat the rilling and waxing process from time to time when the base starts to show signs of becoming too smooth, or when the dry, oxidized surface on the base needs to be removed.

Stone Grinding

Will rilling eliminate the stone grinder structure on the base? Yes. But does it matter? No.

Many ski companies' racing models are offered with bases "patterned" from a base finishing process done by a stone grinder. By holding the ski toward a light source and sighting along the base, a pattern can be seen. These patterns can be beneficial for speed on alpine racing skis. But stone ground bases have not proven advantageous in cross-country. It appears the speeds are not high enough and the ski pressure on the snow is too great.

Rilling and/or sanding with silicon carbide sandpaper appears to offer better results from cross-country skis in improving glide. There is some evidence that a broken rilling structure rather than parallel lines may be a better method, but there would be an advantage only at high speeds.

A few suppliers are rilling their klister skis at the factory. new skis can be rilled just as they are when they come from the factory, but the preferred method is as follows:

1. Clean the base with wax remover, even if the skis are new.

2. Sand the base with #100 grit paper until all high and low spots and grinder oscillation marks have been removed and the base has an even sanding pattern. Work from tip to tail.

3. Buff the base with Fibertex.

4. Rill the base with the bar or riller tool.

5. Buff lightly again with Fibertex.

6. Follow the recommended waxing procedures.

The textured surface will help release surface tension and reduce friction to keep the skis gliding freely over some of the snow surfaces that have been most difficult to handle. Individual skiers may want to experiment with structuring skis. These techniques will provide better performance for the average skier, particularly for skiers who have neglected their skis.

Whatever the rilling process used, it is very important that it be followed up with Fibertex buffing and a wire brush to obtain the desired clean, open base. This removes the microscopic polyethylene fibers and burrs raised by the structuring process. Switch back and forth between Fibertex and the brush two or three times. Finally, wax, scrape, and once again lightly wire brush the skis to reemphasize the structure acquired. Occasionally during the season, the structuring process can be repeated when the skis feel slower than usual or when the base becomes too smooth, nicked, or burred.

26 Cross-Country Boot-Binding Systems

Although current cross-country ski boots and bindings are not as complicated and costly as their alpine counterparts, they are designed to do more than hold your toes in place on a skinny ski. Fortunately for the industry and the sport, today's equipment is built for performance and control.

The current word in boots and bindings is "systems." Systems are "proprietary," that is, their components are not interchangeable with other systems. The first system was the 75mm three-pin Nordic Norm that attempted to standardize mounting screw placement, boot width and thickness, and pin placement. But standard does not mean adequate. New designs began trickling down from international racing as soon as trail grooming began to improve.

Boots and bindings were narrowed to 50mm to reduce drag on the new, firmer, deeper tracks. Notches were cut in boot heels to mate with wedge-shaped heel plates for better downhill control.

Then Adidas did away with pins altogether when they introduced the first modern boot-binding system at the 1976 Olympic Games. Although the system had some initial glitches (one hapless Russian paddled along on one ski in the men's relay), it became de rigueur equipment for a majority of racers.

Salomon developed a system with their SR 90 racing boot binding, which was the first to place the hinge material on the binding rather than the boot. That made replacing the part of the system most susceptible to breakage and wear a $5 proposition rather than a $90 tragedy. Salomon introduced a touring boot a year later and entered the cross-country market so aggressively that they became the dominant company in the industry.

Although different enough to preclude interchangeability, today's systems must address similar design and performance parameters. Here, roughly, are the factors that must be considered when designing a system.

Forward Flex: The distance the boot heel can be lifted from the ski before lifting the ski tail off the snow.

Break Point: The place where the boot bends during forward flexing.

Lateral Stability: The ability of the system to place the boot heel squarely on the heel plate after each forward flex, especially when side-loaded as in the herringbone or skating step.

Torsional Stability: The ability of the system to translate foot commands to the ski's edges when the boot is twisted in the binding as in snowplow turning.

Ski Return: The speed and degree to which the system returns the ski to the boot after forward flexing. Most often a concern when skating.

Boot Retention: The ability of the binding to hold the boot on the ski during all phases of skiing.

Ease of Entry and Release: Sounds simple, but stranger things have happened than a binding that would not close or open on demand.

Toss in a few other obvious items such as boot fit, boot comfort, choice of materials, and system styling, and you have a basic picture of the challenge. Understandably, the components of each system which address these design parameters share some similarities. Here are some common features:

Hinge Point: This is where the system flexes forward. There are two types: (1) the flex plate, which incorporates a flexible, usually plastic, material on either the boot (75mm Nordic Norm or original Adidas) or the binding (Salomon Nordic System), and (2) the fixed axis, which uses a true mechanical hinge with a fixed axis on the binding (NNN, SDS, Contact, and Tyrolia).

Flex Control: Each system has a device for limiting forward flex to a desired amount. Salomon SNS uses variable thickness flex plates, Adidas SDS uses springs, while NNN, Contact,

and Tyrolia use various bumpers commonly called flex nubs. The flex control device also serves to return the ski to the boot when skating or performing the herringbone step.

Bridge Plate: Most current systems incorporate a sole plate mounted on the ski just behind the toe piece which mates with a groove or grooves molded in the boot sole. This improves lateral stability even when the heel is partially disengaged from the heel plate.

Heel Plate: Mounted under the boot heel, the heel plate may be wedge shaped to mate with a notch in the boot heel or consist of several sharp spikes that press into a soft boot heel pad.

In looking at the specific boot-binding systems on the market today, each has positive and negative features that should be considered when making a choice. The catch-all phrase for the Contact system is "low-budget fixed axis." Two notches molded into the boot sole fit into corresponding tabs on the binding. The hinged binding's forward flex is limited by a replaceable flex nub. Soft nubs allow greater heel lift for accomplished diagonal striders, while harder nubs are available for beginning skiers looking for maximum lateral stability on downhills and skaters who desire lateral stability and a fast ski return.

The nubs are user serviceable with nothing more than a flat screwdriver blade to pry them out. The sole plate has a single, peaked ridge, and the heel plate is of the spiked variety.

The plastic boot/binding interface is sloppier than the metal-to-metal type used by other systems and, unfortunately, becomes sloppier with wear. This reduces the system's lateral and

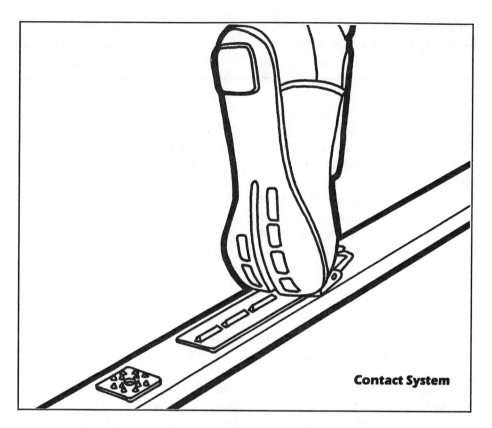

Contact System

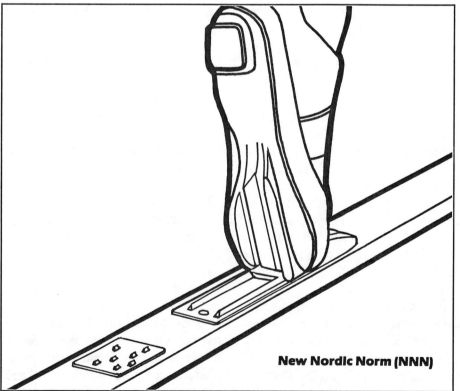

New Nordic Norm (NNN)

torsional stability, especially for advanced, aggressive skiers. But since the system is relatively economical, it is a far superior choice over the ancient 75mm Nordic Norm system for beginner packages.

The New Nordic Norm (NNN) is a system packed with innovations. First, its hinge pivots on a bar incorporated onto the boot directly under the toes. In other words, the hinge pin is on the boot, while the bracket is on the binding. The pivot point's close proximity to the toes gives the skier a feeling of quicker ski control than with systems that place the pivot point farther forward.

Imagine a sailboat rudder with a four-foot tiller. With your hand on the end of the tiller, move the tiller through its complete arc. Then try it with your hand two feet in from the end. With your hand halfway down the tiller, you will swing a shorter arc for the same amount of rudder movement. The NNN system's closer pivot point, like the abbreviated tiller, turns the ski with less leg rotation than other systems.

The ridge plate incorporates two parallel ridges that merge into a single block just behind the toe piece. The solid block portion near the pivot point rises higher off the ski than the dual ridges, providing lateral and torsional stability even when the hinge is fully flexed. Forward flex is limited by an interchangeable flex nub available in various densities. The heel plate is of the spiked variety.

Rottefella manufactures both a step-in recreational binding and a manual racing binding for the New Nordic Norm. The bindings look a little crude in spite of their paramount flex and stability characteristics.

NNN boots are available from a number of different manufacturers.

The Salomon Nordic System (SNS) is the most popular system in this country. Except for their latest racing bindings, the system has remained virtually unchanged since its market debut. A D-ring molded into the boot's toe clamps to a plastic flex plate housed in a metal or plastic binding toe piece. Flex is tuned by installing thinner or thicker flex plates held in place by the front binding screw.

A single ridge sole plate and spiked heel plate provide lateral control. Although forward flex characteristics are comparable to fixed axis systems, lateral and torsional stability suffer with this flex plate design, especially when the heel is disengaged from the heel plate.

A newer racing version differs from this pattern by using only two screws to anchor the flex plate and binding. It requires extra care (epoxy on the ridge plate and in the screw holes) when installed on delicate racing skis. A third screw holds the binding at the ridge plate. The skating binding has a metal cap that presses on top of the flex plate for additional torsional stability. Salomon offers a two-drawer dealer service kit with extra boot and binding parts and insole materials for custom fitting.

The Skating Diagonal System (SDS) is Adidas' third generation system. Its most unique feature is its use of coil springs for limiting forward flex and returning the ski. There are two springs in each fixed axis binding that can be mixed and matched to achieve the desired tension. In use, SDS allows so much forward flex that the boot can be raised to 45 degrees before breaking at the ball of the foot or

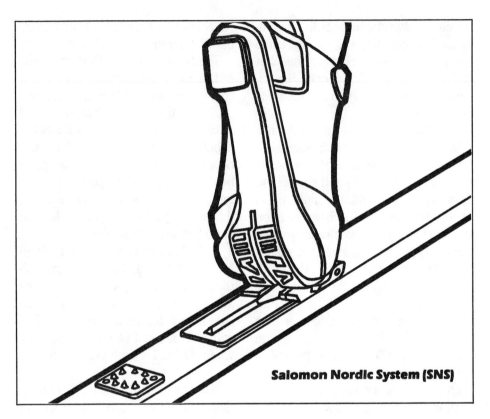

Salomon Nordic System (SNS)

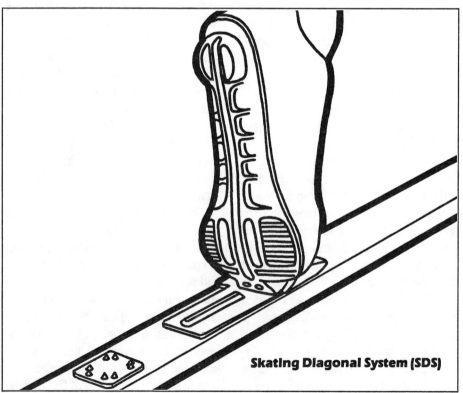

Skating Diagonal System (SDS)

lifting the ski tail off the snow (but not at the expense of lateral or torsional stability). The hinge mechanism uses metal-to-metal contact (like scissors) that ensures precise movement.

The stiffest springs limit forward flex only slightly more than the softest springs. The difference is the amount of resistance encountered during flexing. A strong, aggressive skier can leave the ski on the snow longer and lengthen his stride more while skating than with a flex plate or flex nub system, yet still expect a fast ski return. Whether this is a technical boon or bane has yet to be proven, but it deserves consideration.

SDS boots have a single groove from nose to tail which mates with a corresponding ridge plate and heel plate. This ridge and precision binding system provides positive lateral control for downhill, turning, and skating maneuvers.

27 *Skating Skis Binding Placement*

With all that has been written about skating technique and its effect on Nordic skiing, it seems there should be a consensus on where to install bindings on skating skis. Yet this is not the case, since what makes a good skating ski is just now being understood and accepted.

With every innovation in sports equipment, athletes must experiment to find the optimal performance capability of the new gear. And over the past few seasons, binding placement has become the subject of many differing theories. A skier who just bought a new pair of skating skis could easily have received up to a half-dozen different opinions on where to install the bindings or why this or that placement was best. The binding manufacturer may have supplied a paper template and general installation rules in the box of bindings but, when pressed for specifics on location, would defer to the ski manufacturer for an answer. Special interest ski magazines further confused the issue with regular reports on new installation ideas which sent already confused skiers to their basements to reinstall their bindings.

The villain in binding location is that old standby—the balance point. Ski shop and home mechanics have trusted the balance point for years. It was home base for Nordic mounting. You found the balance point and made sure the three pins on your old-style bindings fell directly over that point. Newer bindings like the Adidas 38mm, Salomon SNS, and others were installed at the same point.

Then came skating and the new boot-binding systems. Skiers found they had too much tip drop or skis that were tail heavy. Skis whose tips caught snow on each skating kick recovery or skis whose glide slowed because of tail drop were a problem.

The search was on for the right binding installation point. Ski manufacturers' recommendations sufficed for a time but not necessarily for skiers switching boot-binding systems. Although ski manufacturers say it in many different ways, they are getting closer to a consensus on where to install bindings on skating skis. The situation with classic skis is clear and easy to understand.

Karhu

Karhu's master technician, Heikki Suominen, has studied the binding placement problem thoroughly. He has produced a set of printed guidelines for Karhu's skating and classic skis. Suominen bases his installation rules on working with the Salomon SNS boot-binding system.

With skating skis, install at the balance point of the skis, which is found using a set formula. Take the Karhu binding installation chart instructions and find by exact measurement the stiffest part of the ski. To this figure, add on a measurement taken from a table which accounts for the size of the boot to be used with the skis. These two figures added together place the binding at the balance point just forward of the stiffest point of the ski.

For example, a pair of Karhu 188-centimeter skating skis would produce an initial measurement of 83 centimeters forward from the ski's tail to the stiffest point of the ski. Mark that point on both skis, then consult the boot size table for a size 41 boot and add an additional 6.5 centimeters. Adding the 6.5 centimeters makes the total distance from the tail of the ski to the ski's balance point 89.5 centimeters. Using an SNS jig, install the bindings over the balance point. This installation assures that you have the bindings situated perfectly so that the ball of the skier's foot pushes down on the stiffest point of the ski.

For classic skis, Suominen recommends mounting directly over the stiffest point of the ski. The same chart used for the skating ski measurement is also used, with modifications, to arrive at the stiffest point for classic skis. According to Suominen, the stiffest point of the ski's camber must be directly under the ball of the foot. It does not matter whether the ski is balanced, tip heavy, or tail heavy. These are matters of perception and do not influence the performance of the ski. What is important is to have the ball of the foot in the right relationship with the ski's camber.

Jarvinen/Adidas

Jarvinen/Adidas' recommendation for a skating ski is to mount the binding 2.5 centimeters ahead of the ski's balance point, and the new Adidas SDS binding jig indicates that point. The company line on classic skis, also shown on the jig, is to mount one centimeter ahead of the balance point.

Rossignol

Rossignol recommends installing at the balance point for both classic and skating skis. But they note that top-level racers are going to experiment with binding placement. According to Rossignol, however, the farther forward the binding on a skating ski, the slower the ski will glide.

Madshus/Fischer/Peltonen

Echoing the same caveat as Rossignol that racers will experiment, all three companies say the balance point is the place to install SNS, SDS, NNN, and TXC bindings. The redesign of skating skis over the past two years has taken a lot of the guesswork out of binding placement. For classic ski binding installation, the rule remains over the highest point of the wax pocket. Fischer's Dan Simoneau and Madshus' Steve Kvinlaug both note that experimentation with placement by top international racers does cause confusion.

The Kleerup Theory

If it is a technical debate, who better to ask for an opinion than Bert Kleerup of Eagle River Research? Kleerup says for skating, get the center of the skier's weight over the center of the ski's pressure distribution point. To do this, squeeze the skis together using a C-clamp placed close to the balance point. Squeeze the clamp down and move it around until the last bit of camber is showing right below the clamp. This is where the ball of the foot should fall on the topsheet. From this test, approximate how far forward of the critical ball-of-the-foot area the binding needs to be installed. Installation does not vary by system if the C-clamp method is used.

Kleerup admits that his system is geared to the better skater. It puts the binding forward of the balance point, which could make the beginning skater feel unstable on his skis. For classic skis, Kleerup says, it is all closely related to the balance point of the skis, but check it against the pressure distribution point to make sure there is not much disparity. Good, classic skis have not changed much in recent years. Manufacturers have the relationship between the balance point and pressure distribution point well located.

Although everyone says it in a slightly different way, it appears there

is a consensus on where to place bindings on classic skis. Find the balance point, and use the binding manufacturer's jig to install. To make doubly sure the balance point is close to the pressure distribution point, squeeze the skis together by hand and check with the naked eye. Often classic skis with the same serial number will have quite different cambers and this may or may not be a problem, depending on the variance.

If the balance points are significantly different, return the skis to the shop or the manufacturer. If they are under half an inch off, shave the tip or tail of one or both skis until they have close to the same balance point. Skating skis also can be shaved if a skier complains of skis that are too tip heavy or tail heavy.

It is far better to shave a ski than move bindings around, which can be dangerous with some of the new airy cores. Kleerup, for example, has tried adding weight in the form of coins to the tails of skis deemed tip heavy with some success. Still, shaving is the better way to rebalance skis.

Which brings us back to how skating bindings should be properly placed on the ski. Karhu makes it an easy "by-the-chart" proposition. Kleerup arrives at almost the same solution using the C-clamp test. Others say to install at the traditional balance point. But they hint that if installed a bit forward of this point, it is more likely the ball of the foot will be over the stiffest part of the ski—in synch with how World Cup ski technicians install bindings.

Lost in all this discussion is how you actually install bindings, whether classic or skating models. As important as where you put the bindings is the drill bit used to penetrate the ski's topsheet and core. A drill bit that is too big will strip holes; one that is too small could crack the binding plate. Use the binding manufacturer's recommended drill bit size. In most cases, it will be a 3.6 millimeter. Use a Posi-drive screwdriver to gently widen the upper portion of the newly drilled hole before installing the screws.

The most important decision to make is not which ski to buy but how to place and mount the bindings on the skis. Do it wrong and even a great pair of skis won't perform properly.

28 *Telemark Bindings*

A common mistake made by well-meaning ski manufacturers, retailers, and ski technicians is thinking that because telemark skis are usually considered to be Nordic skis, their bindings should be mounted according to Nordic criteria. But unless you use telemark skis mostly for touring (and they are a slow, heavy choice for kicking and gliding), you should know that telemark skis are designed and used more like alpine skis than Nordic skis. Consider them "skinny" alpine skis.

The Nordic definition of the balance point for a ski is the point on the ski where it can be balanced on a sharp edge, say, a scraper in a vise. Many skiers and manufacturers use the balance point as a criteria for binding placement on cross-country skis used for touring and racing. But the balance point has little to do with telemark skis. Telemark skis are meant to be skied on their edges, not gliding flat down a prepared track. The criteria for mounting telemark bindings should be the ski's edges—the ski's sidecut. As with an alpine ski, you want the ball of your foot over the center of the running surface. Since alpine equipment is much more standardized, especially the boots, alpine ski technicians enjoy the advantage of an excellent system of positioning marks molded and silk screened on the boots and skis.

The Mid-Chord Position

For years, alpine ski manufacturers have used, and some still do use the ski's mid-chord as the spot for boot location. Mid-chord (or half-chord or chord-center) is half the distance from the ski's tip to its tail measured in a straight line. The standard placement of the binding is with boot toe on the half-chord.

But this is just a place to start. Alpine racers deviate from this chord-center norm for different racing skis and according to personal preference. Giant slalom skiers generally mount their boot toes dead on chord-center. Slalom skiers, who want their skis to be very quick turning, mount their boot toes one centimeter ahead of chord-center. Downhillers, whose skis should run straight and stable, mount their skis with the boot toes a centimeter back from chord-center.

Binding Placement

First check to see what the manufacturer recommends for binding placement. They know their own products best and might have done some testing that could give you valuable information on how to get the best performance out of their skis. They may have made special design considerations for their binding location which are not obvious to the consumer, such as low-profile tips.

If they mention anything about balance point, be skeptical. Discuss the options with the manufacturer and see if they have any reason to disagree with a different binding location. Usually with telemark skis, they do not. The recommendation for mounting telemark bindings is locating the pins (boot toe) on half-chord.

Mounting

These are the steps to take to mount a pair of telemark skis on chord-center. Find the ski's chord length. Measure the distance in a straight line from the ski's tip to its tail. Now divide the distance in half. Measure that half-distance from the ski tail and mark it on the ski. After marking both skis, double-check your half-chord from the tips. The marks should be equidistant from the tip and tail of the ski.

This mark is where you want the binding pins, which, according to Nordic Norm, should be located directly under the boot toe. Using either the paper template included with the binding or, preferably, a metal shop jig, lo-cate the mark for the pins over the half-chord mark. If you use a shop jig, be sure that the hole spacing corresponds to your bindings. There is a regular Nordic Norm, and the new Telemark Norm, which spaces the front hole and the rear holes farther apart.

If you want to use the bindings with more than one pair of boots, jig-mount them. Drill the three holes, tap the holes with a No. 12 ski-service tap, and mount the bindings. Be sure to use the drill size recommended by the ski manufacturer.

Should you want to be more exact and custom mount your bindings for just one pair of boots, drill only the rear holes. Be sure to use a rear hole instead of one of the front ones. This way you will not get a hole too close to a side wall.

Tap the hole with a standard No. 12 ski-shop tap. Mount the binding care-fully with this one screw, tightening the screw. Put the boot carefully in the binding and turn it back and forth until it is centered on the ski. (A mark in the center of the backstay will make it easier to eyeball this centering process.)

Once you are confident that the boot is centered, carefully remove the boot from the binding and mark the undrilled holes. Remove the binding, drill and tap the holes, and you are ready to remount it. You can fine-tune the centering of the boot by experimenting with the screws, tightening them in different order.

Accommodating Bigger or Smaller Boots

There is one hitch in the boot toe on half-chord mounting standard. What about skiers who use the same length ski but have very different length boots?

To take care of this situation, alpine ski manufacturers have ingeniously developed a mid-boot system, using the average-size boot. They determined where they wanted this average-size boot to be on a ski, then came up with a system that automatically determined the proper placement on the ski for smaller or larger boots.

For an alpine technician, this is quite simple. Most manufacturers mark their boot soles in the middle with a line or arrow. (Some deviate a centimeter for different performance, but half-boot is standard.) The ski has a mid-boot mark, too, usually both on the silk screened graphics and as a little arrow on the side wall. Since the average boot sole is 30-centimeters, the mid-boot designation on the ski should be 15 centimeters behind the ski's half-chord. Mount a 30-centimeter boot using the corresponding ski and boot marks, and the boot's toes should fall on the half-chord.

This is a guideline. Some ski and boot manufacturers deviate from this norm for various design purposes. But for consumers and ski mechanics, if you understand the guidelines, it is easier to deal with deviations from this norm.

With bigger and smaller boots, the mid-boot system takes care of positioning on the ski. It splits the difference between the norm of 30 centimeters for a boot and the actual boot sole length. Let us say that your 32-centimeter boot has a mid-boot mark at 16 centimeters. When mounting it on the ski's mid-boot mark, its toe will be one centimeter ahead of half-chord.

If the sole length is 28 centimeters, then the toe will be one centimeter behind half-chord. The center of the boot is always positioned correctly on the ski, regardless of boot size.

Accommodating Different-Size Telemark Boots

How does this mid-boot business apply to telemark skis? This system makes it possible to be accurate in locating telemark boots, considering that you are working with handmade leather boots that usually vary in length (due to the human element) in the manufacturing process. For most skiers, use the simple boot toe on half-chord method. But, if you want to be really exact, especially if you have unusually large or small feet, then you can apply the mid-boot principle described above.

Begin by measuring the boot. Figure the difference in your sole length from the 30-centimeter norm, noting whether it is longer or shorter. Next, divide this difference in half and write it down. Now locate the boot toe mark of the mounting jig. This is half-distance either ahead of or behind your half-chord mark.

For boots longer than 30 centimeters, the mark will be ahead of the half-chord mark; for those shorter than 30 centimeters, it will be behind it. For example, for a 32-centimeter boot, you want to mount the boot with its toe one centimeter ahead of half-chord. For a 28-centimeter boot, you want the toe one centimeter behind the half-chord.

Before drilling any holes, check your work. Put your boot on the ski in the location you have determined.

Measure and mark (on the side of the sole) the center of the boot sole. For a 30-centimeter boot, this mark should fall 15 centimeters behind the mid-chord mark. If it is not, start over. Be sure that longer boots are forward of the mid-chord, shorter boots behind. Once you are sure you have all of your marks in the right place, drill, tap and screw, using the rear hole first.

Mounting Nordic skis this way can be tricky, especially since Nordic mounting instructions refer to the boot toe and the pins, not the mid-boot. But if you are so inclined, persevere and you can be as exacting as any alpine ski mechanic. If you use this approach, note that Nordic bindings grab the boot only at the toe. Anyone who uses your skis who has feet of very different sizes will not have the advantage of your precision binding mounting.

If all this boot-center business seems too complicated, do not worry about it for your Nordic boots. Simply mount the boot toe on mid-chord as first described. You will be a lot closer than the old-fashioned balance point method.

PART **V** *ALPINE POLES*

29 *Basic Pole Construction*

The pole plant is the starting point for every turn, so a good pole must be able to be planted quickly and easily. This is accomplished by using a pole with a strong, light shaft and a light tip. The lighter tip is achieved by tapering, or "swaging," the pole downward and keeping the balance point as close to the grip as possible. Swaging takes advantage of the old leverage law of physics: weight increases as the distance from the source of power increases.

Tapering the shaft at the most distant area from the hand (power source) produces the lightest possible swing weight. It is possible to check the swing weight of individual poles by actually swinging different poles in each hand. Since the object is to plant the pole as quickly as possible, swing the pole back and forth with a flick of the wrist. The skier should wear a pair of gloves when selecting poles as this offers a chance to check the fit of the grip.

Most poles are manufactured with straight shafts, but a few are being produced with shafts bent just under the grips. The purpose is to require less arm and wrist motion, which enables a skier to keep the upper body more erect. It also allows for planting the pole farther downhill, helping to initiate a faster, smoother turn.

The four parts of a ski pole that should be evaluated for suitability for the individual skier are the shaft, the grip, the tip, and the basket.

Shaft

The major difference in ski poles is the shaft. Its strength and durability is determined by the alloy, outside diameter, wall thickness, and construction. Shafts may be constructed using either seamless or welded tubing. Seamless shafts are the strongest and most expensive to produce. An ingot of aluminum is drawn over a mandrel (spindle) to mold the aluminum into a hollow tube. This procedure is repeated until the desired diameter and wall thickness is achieved. A welded shaft is constructed by taking a flat sheet of aluminum with the desired wall thickness, rolling it into a tube, and welding the seam together. The outside weld is invisible to the naked eye.

The only way to determine if a shaft is welded or seamless is to look at the inner wall of the shaft. If no weld line is visible, it is seamless. A seamless tube is normally stronger than a welded tube. If shafts are swaged, seamless aluminum tubes are not automatically stronger.

Manufacturers working with sheet aluminum claim it is easier to produce a uniform aluminum alloy in a flat sheet. For that reason, most pole manufacturers start with a flat sheet, roll it, weld it, and then do the swaging.

The desired shaft material must be the lightest, strongest available. For over twenty-five years, aluminum alloys have been the choice of the ski pole industry. Different manufacturers sprang up with new concepts, configurations, and cosmetics, but aluminum is used exclusively to produce alpine poles.

There are almost as many primary sources of aluminum as there are ski pole manufacturers. To designate different grades or composition of alloys, the American Aluminum Association (AAA) assigns reference numbers. Alloys within a series (e.g., 7001, 7075, 7020) are similar in composition of elements such as copper, zinc, magnesium, silicon, chromium, but the percentage of each element is different. The 7000 series aluminum alloys are thinner and lighter and resist twice the force without bending or breaking as a shaft wall made from 5086 aluminum alloy.

The top-of-the-line poles are made with 7000 series alloys. The 7001 alloy is the lightest and strongest.

Most inexpensive poles are made with 5000 or 6000 alloys. According to AAA, it does not matter whether 7075 aluminum is obtained from Picheney, France, Laval in Italy, Easton in the United States or a prime supplier in any other country. If it has the AAA series number assigned, it will be the same aluminum alloy. The difference will be the price in American dollars.

Although specific alloys are recognized as the lightest and strongest, not all manufacturers of quality poles select the same materials. It is possible to determine the aluminum alloy used to produce a pole by checking the hang tag or looking for a mark on the pole.

In addition to the alloy selected, wall thickness and the diameter of the shaft also determine strength and durability. The larger the outside diameter, the stronger the pole. A mere reduction in diameter from 19 mm to 18 mm will reduce the shaft strength by 10 percent.

Walls are usually 0.8 mm at the thickest point. Rossignol's John Douglas said some racers are using poles with outside diameters of 19 mm because they are more durable. Durability is more important to them than 10 percent less weight.

Tapering the shaft is what produces its swing weight flexibility. As the shaft is tapered, the outside diameter is reduced. But the mass of material is condensed as the shaft is tapered, so the wall thickness in the tapered area is increased or the length is increased.

Grip

A skier has the option of choosing a universal grip (the pole can be used in either hand), platform grip, pistol grip, ribbed grip, or fluted grip. One advantage of the universal grip is that a pole can be carried in either hand. This randomly distributes the nicks caused by the steel edges of skis, which can weaken the shaft. The advantage of a custom grip, with a left and right pole, is that the grip usually is more form fitting.

Grips can have standard straps or breakaway or safety straps that will release if the skier snags a basket. Whether to go strapless or with straps is up to the individual skier. A strapless grip is favored by skiers who want a positive reacting pole for quick pole plants. The notched grip with a strap, the "pistol grip" style, is the choice of competitors and skiers who want a wide range of motion. A basic grip with a strap falls somewhere in-between.

Tip

For years, ski pole tips have been pointed. Now manufacturers are changing to steel conical tips for safety. They are case hardened for durability and hollow ground for lightness. The 360-degree concave shape provides a superior cutting edge to the 4- or 6-point ice tip. Some tips have concave cups with serrated edges inside the smooth outside edges so they will not catch on clothing. The pointed tip is found only on a few less expensive poles.

Basket

Space-age plastics are used in ski pole baskets for lightness and flexibility in coldest of temperatures. Hytrel and Elvax from Du Pont are two of the registered trademark plastics used. Small disk baskets are favored by competitors and skiers who ski most often on packed snow and who want the lightest possible weight at the tip of their pole. As the weight of the basket is near the end of the pole, each fraction of an ounce added to, or taken away from, the weight at the end has a compounding effect on the swing weight of the pole.

Bench Tips

Ski Tech magazine invites its reachers to contribute tips on new tools they may have created or new and better ways of working with ski equipment at home or in the shop. Below are some of these readers' contributions.

Repairing Along the Edge

When we have a hard time putting new base material along a metal edge, we clean the metal with 100-grit emery paper or a brass pad to get all the rust off. Then we use wax remover to clean the area. Then we blow the area with 60 psi air.

With care, we brush an anaerobic-type contact cement on the area, trying not to get cement on the old base. (Use a very small amount so there are no globs.)

When the cement gets tacky, use your base extruder gun to fill in the bad sections. If it has air bubbles, use a ½-inch or ¾-inch chisel to force out bubbles while the base material is still hot. You may have to put base material on two or three times before it comes out right.

Surform down and it's ready for stone grinding. It takes practice, but you can get perfect welds—they just don't look very good.

Dennis Buckingham
Mt. Ski Tuning & Repair
Lake Tahoe, California

A No-Spill Container

Our shop does a high number of tune-ups every year, ranging from quick sharpen and wax jobs to full service stone grinding. Our biggest problem stems from being in the East where we use a lot of snow-making equipment.

The majority of ski bases we see are usually covered with grime and dirt, which makes them difficult to wax effectively. We have found a very quick, easy method of cleaning ski bases. Take a one liter plastic soda bottle (we prefer Welch's Grape) and with a small finish nail, poke several holes in the screw-on top.

142

Fill the bottle with wax remover or denatured alcohol and you have a no-spill container that you can squeeze to regulate the amount of liquid you want to use.

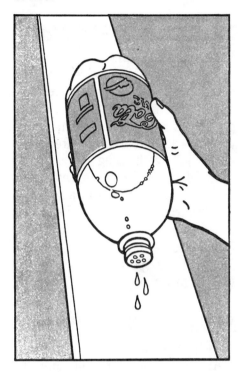

(Regarding the ongoing debate about brake retainers, the best, most effective one we've found comes out of a vacuum cleaner. For some of the Hoover models, there is a small rubber drive belt that stretches just enough to pull over a ski brake. It is thick enough not to rip and inexpensive enough that you can get thousands of them without spending a lot of money.)
Rick Fincher, Service Manager
Darien Sport Shop
Bridgeport, Connecticut

Reusing Plastic Bags

Many ski companies package their skis in long plastic bags to protect them during shipping. Instead of throwing the bags away, they can be used to present a finished product to your customer.

Simply cut the bags into 12- to 14-inch lengths and slip one section over the tip and one over the tail of one ski following a tune-up. This protects the skis and the work you have just finished while giving your customer something extra at no cost to you.

Considering the number of "covers" you can make from one bag, an average shop's ski order should produce a supply of covers that will last an entire season. (They can be stretched farther by cutting the bag lengthwise before cutting them into sections.)
Peter J. Faletto
Al's Sporting Goods
Logan, Utah

Open Wider

I use a dentist's pick to prepare a ski base for P-tex repair. Then I use compressed air from a can to clean away the loose material.

Cleaning gouges before using the P-tex gun makes a more durable repair.
Carolyn Graff
Poughkeepsie, New York

Files for Beveling

Most beveling tools require small files that fit into the tool. These small files dull quickly and are rather expensive to buy.

To make your own files that will fit a beveling tool, simply put a new file in a vise so that the size you need sticks out from the vise. Take a hammer and strike the protruding piece. Presto, the length of file needed for the beveling tool breaks off and can be used in the tool.

Brian McQueen
Banff, Alberta

Ski Bottom Grooving

Repairing a damaged groove is difficult without the use of an expensive machine. I find that the best way to repair a damaged groove is to press out the excess P-tex before it hardens. For round grooves (Atomic), drip P-tex into the damaged area, then immediately press the excess P-tex out, using something with the same curvature as the groove (Bic pens work well for this).

Keep applying pressure until the P-tex has hardened. This should leave the groove smooth and in its original shape around the damaged area. For skis with square grooves (Rossignol), cut a popsicle stick lengthwise to match the width of the groove and follow the same procedure as above.

Mark Grove
Turning Point Sports
Copper Mountain, Colorado

Untangling Cords

One problem that frequently occurred in our shop was dealing with electrical extension cords. The life of the heat guns, waxers, drills, and other power tools depends on them.

I found that suspending self-winding cords from various strategic locations throughout the shop solved the problem. The extension cords are always within reach, and you don't have to worry about putting them away. No more tripping over cords unless you walk on the ceiling.

Jay Vorobel
Harborside Sports Adventures
Birmingham, Michigan

Protecting Welds

When filling in base welds along the edge, P-tex often hangs out over the edge. Sometimes this can present a problem when shaving them down with a Surform tool. More often than not, the overhanging P-tex gets snagged by the Surform and tears out. To prevent this, use an X-acto knife to trim off the excess P-tex before filing.

Mark Grove
Turning Point Sports
Copper Mountain, Colorado

A Tidy Bench

As a household ski technician, I am always searching for new ways to store screwdrivers, drill bits, snow thermometers, and so forth, without taking up a lot of room on my small ski bench. What I have done is to make holes in the corners of my bench about ½ inch in diameter and place the tools in the holes. They are neat, attractive, and great for a technician with little room for spare tools.

Bryan Risley
Madison, Connecticut

Filing Bench Files

There is an easy way to keep your tuning bench less cluttered. If you use several files, you will want to keep them handy as well as sharp. Simply drill holes in your bench and place the tang end of the files in the holes.

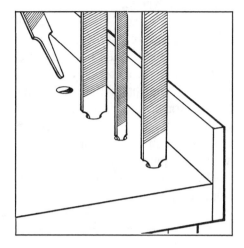

The teeth of the file will not get dull from placing it flat on the bench. This is also an alternative to having them weigh down your shop apron.

David Doherty
Boulder, Colorado

Making Your Own Vise

Not all home ski mechanics want to invest in a special ski vise, but trying to use a carpenter's vise is rarely satisfactory. I have a suggestion for a homemade ski vise that is secure, does not damage the side walls of the ski, and even gets the ski brakes out of the way.

The trick is to first fashion a boot sole from two pieces of scrap two-by-four. Trace the boot sole outline on one piece, cut it out with a jig saw, and trim the front end and rear to get the proper toe and heel height.

Then add a second piece of two-by-four to the top of the first. The finished wooden sole will fit in the ski binding in place of the boot.

With the wooden sole in the binding, you can then invert the ski and se-cure the attached two-by-four (not the ski side walls) in any carpenter's vise with as much force as necessary.

I use the system with a portable Workmate-type bench to secure the sides of the two-by-four and add support strips at the ends of the bench to support the ends of the ski. This has worked as well as any ski vise, and there is no problem with slanted side walls.

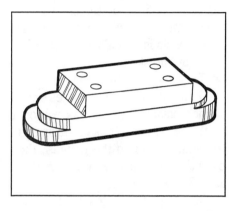

Granted, you have to fashion a wooden boot sole for each size boot shell to fit into the binding of the ski you want to tune, but this is no problem for personal or family use. Try it. It works.

Steve Christensen
Midland, Michigan

Prevent Hooking

If you feel your skis hooking or grabbing too soon when starting your turn, try beveling the tip a little more. Bevel four to six inches starting from just ahead of the running surface. Lightly brush off the sharpening burr with fine emery cloth.

This method keeps the tip of the ski working the way it was designed to work. If you feel you also need to dull the tips, use emery cloth or a few brushes with a sharpening stone. Take care not to round the edge so it can't be resharpened again if you wish.

Danny Brienza
Looney Tunes Ski Repair
Taos Ski Valley, New Mexico

Using Brass Pads

When preparing a base to make a P-tex repair, I first run the ski over the stone grinder to see how flat the ski is. If the ski is in really bad condition, I true up the ski on the wet belt sander. This roughens the base.

Then I clean out the gouges with a ¼-inch chisel. I spray wax remover on the base, use a brass scouring pad to clean down into the gouges, then blow the base clean with compressed air—60 pounds plus.

This way, new P-tex holds better and won't pull out when I use a Surform to clean off the excess P-tex. This method works when repairing the new sintered or Electra bases. The main problem with the new racing bases is that if not properly cleaned, the P-tex will not adhere.

I find a brass pad is excellent to clean out the gouges and to cut away any excess P-tex hair. I also find that if the brass pad is used with a little extra pressure prior to waxing, the pad will put some structure into the base to help produce a better wax job.

Dennis Buckingham
Mountain Ski Tuning & Repair
Tahoma, California

C-Clamp Vises

If you can't justify the expense of buying a ski vise for at-home tuning (or if you have to improvise), any standard vise mounted on the end of a workbench will do.

I fasten a small C-clamp to the tail of a ski (protecting the ski with small wooden blocks). Then I clamp the C-clamp into my workbench vise. If you adjust the height of the tail so that both the tip of the ski and the heel unit of the binding rest on the workbench, you have a firm ski to press against while scraping. This works equally well with new trapezoid skis and conventional skis.

This method can also be used on the road. Carry an extra C-clamp in your tuning kit. You can use it, for example, to clamp the first C-clamp to a chair leg or any other object that will offer some stability. While not as sturdy as the workbench method, it works perfectly for light tuning and waxing.

Gary S. Haffke, P.E.
Carrollton, Virginia

Try a Surform Rasp

We've developed a somewhat different process for repairing bases and detuning skis. After applying P-tex to fill gouges and scratches, we use a Surform rasp instead of going after the excess with a metal scraper.

A metal scraper can skip and hop over the base, which creates ripples. The Surform produces a smooth, level base.

After grinding the base, sharpening and deburring the edges (with a block of wood), we mark the contact points at the tip and the tail. Then, from the upper contact point to the very tip of the ski, and from the lower contact point to the very end of the ski, we round off the edges with a file.

For about three centimeters from the contact points toward the middle of the ski, we use emery cloth to aggressively rub down the edges. Then we make a light pass over the rest of the edge between the contact points with the emery cloth.

With this process, we set up a smooth transition between the various zones of the edges. When using emery cloth, it is important to wrap it around a file. If you apply pressure with your hand or thumb, you can round off the edges accidentally.

Finally, after waxing, we recommend using only a plastic scraper. A metal scraper can put striations and nicks in the edges and base you have worked so hard to get just right.

Mark Martz
Santa Fe, New Mexico

No More Burns

The last time I burned my fingers while applying hot P-tex to the bases of my skis, it finally made me realize that there must be a safer way.

One trip through the toolbox produced the solution—baby vise grips. The 5-inch size is perfect.

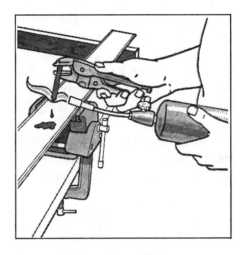

If you hold the P-tex with the vise grips instead of your fingers, you benefit by no more burnt fingers, less waste of P-tex, and much safer working conditions.

Ed Keim
Mechanicsburg, Pennsylvania

Dulling Tips

When I want to dull the tips and tails on a pair of skis, I use a stone or emery cloth. A file tends to round the edges and makes it more difficult to sharpen the edge again. You dull the edges mainly to avoid having the tails or tips catch or grab at the extremes. A stone or emery cloth will take enough sharpness off to keep your skis turning smoothly. If you've dulled them down too far, you can easily sharpen them again.

Dan Brienza
Taos, New Mexico

P-tex and Soda

I've discovered another method to help reduce carbon while P-texing which works very well for me.

As carbon begins to develop, by rolling the P-tex candle on the side of a soda can, the carbon is easily removed. The aluminum can dissipates the heat, allowing a clear flow. It also controls the flame of the candle. Repeat this procedure as often as necessary to keep the carbon down.

When a customer pays me good money to redo the base of his or her skis, I like the skis to go back looking

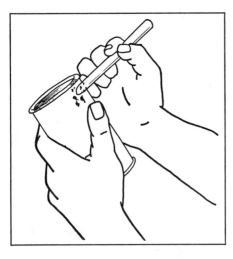

as good as new. By following this simple procedure, it helps me accomplish this.

Maria Gleason
Jay, Vermont

Patching with Epoxy

I've used this easy and permanent method of repairing deep gouges in alpine ski bases for years. I use a mixture of five-minute epoxy and residual base material (produced while scraping down the base during a tune-up session).

To start, trim the base material around the gouged area so that it is clean and leaves a square edge between the damaged area and the original running surface. Remove all loose base material in the area to be repaired. I use an X-acto knife to make the cut and a dental scraper to clean the damaged area.

After cleaning, fill the damaged area to approximately 1/16 to 3/32 of an inch above the base with a 50-50 mixture of five-minute epoxy and base shavings. If possible, let the patch cure overnight. When it has cured completely, gently file the patched area smooth and level with the original base.

If done correctly, the patch will closely match the color of the original base and will last the life of the ski. To keep a ready supply of base material, I make a habit of keeping a small jar of clean base shavings in my toolbox.

James F. Vigani, P.E.
Somerville, New Jersey

Knives

I have one tool I use that works well for trimming away damaged base material when I'm making base repairs. I take a regular carpet knife and cut the curved point off to give me a round blade.

It's common to use an X-acto knife to clean up the base. But I work along the edge of the damaged area using a rocking motion with the rounded end of the carpet knife. I find I have more control and can make cleaner cuts.

I modified my first carpet knife ten

years ago, and I haven't found anything else that works any better.

Dan Brienza
Taos, New Mexico

Neat Benches

Tired of sweeping wax off the floor? Mount a section of rain gutter (like the stuff on the roof of your house) on the edge of your wax bench and leave one end open.

You can sweep wax shavings off the bench into the gutter, then sweep

them out the open end of the gutter into a wastebasket.

No more wax ground into the floor. Clean shops are more productive.

Tom Chelstrom
St. Paul, Minnesota

Advanced Taping

When I'm getting ready to tune a pair of skis and I want to tape my fingers, the first thing I do is run two strips of masking tape, one at a time, over the fingerprint area, up across the end of the finger, and over the nail to just past the first knuckle.

Then I wrap about two turns of tape around the ends of each finger—across the tape I've already put on. The reason I run tape up above the knuckle is that when I'm finished working, I have a pull tab to remove the tape.

When you're tuning skis, you have a choice of wearing gloves or using tape. I believe tape gives you a better feel for what you're doing. The tape is good protection.

Without protection, you're going to end up wearing away your fingernail. If you're doing a number of pairs of skis, without the tape, you wear away the skin. Your fingertips can become very sore, especially if you're using body files.

When I am filing side edges, I hold the file so my fingers go along the sides of the ski and rub directly along the edge so I keep contact and have good control.

For side filing, I only use my strong hand. Picture the ski in a vise on its side, base away from you. I do one edge tip to tail, then I do the other edge tail to tip. That way I can always keep the same pressure on the file. I

don't worry about striations, because I take care of them by smoothing off the edge with a whetstone and paper (220 grit silicone carbide paper).
Ed Chase
Vashon, Washington

Shoe Goo Boot Repair

When I was still racing, I used neoprene pads and other types of foam to modify and fit my boots. I found that sticky-backed pads or pads put on with contact cement would only hold for a short time. The pads would tear when you took your liners out so they could dry.

We started using Shoe Goo or one of the similar shoe repair materials you can buy in a tube at any running store. Shoe Goo really adheres to the liner. You can use it directly on the liner to make minor fit adjustments and then build up coats as the liner loosens during the year. It's almost indestructible.

For major boot work, we used the thinnest neoprene we could find and used Shoe Goo to attach an "L" pad or doughnut, using it just like contact cement.

Once the pad was in place, we would put one or two coats over the pad. That way, when you were taking the liner in or out, it would never tear off.

Anyone who skis 30 or 40 days a year is going to get some kind of liner wear. Using Shoe Goo is the best way I've found to repair minor tears or seam separations. If the stitching looks like it may come apart, spread a couple of layers over the seam, and it will probably solve the problem for the rest of the year.

The running shoe repair materials are flexible, waterproof, and hard to destroy. They're best for personal fittings. They're not too practical for shops because they are not quick drying. Shoe Goo is a good item to carry with you when you go skiing.
Jim Bergh
Boulder, Colorado

Basket Works

There are several ways to take most standard new-style baskets off ski poles. To remove a basket, use a pair of vise grips or a crescent wrench adjusted to the diameter of the pole. Slide the jaws of the wrench over the top of the basket and tap the basket off with a rubber mallet or a hammer.

To tap baskets on, you can use the crescent wrench or vise-grips idea or cut a 5- or 6-inch section of an old pole which can be slipped over the end of the pole and used to secure the basket by tapping the basket on.

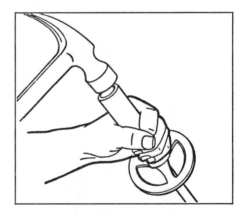

The best method is to make a basket tapper of your own. This is how it looks and is designed.
David Harrison
Flamingo Sports
Seattle, Washington

Index

Other Books from John Muir Publications

22 Days Series
These pocket-size itineraries are a refreshing departure from ordinary guidebooks. Each author has an in-depth knowledge of the region covered and offers 22 tested daily itineraries through their favorite destinations. Included are not only "must see" attractions but also little-known villages and hidden "jewels" as well as valuable general information.

22 Days Around the World by R. Rapoport and B. Willes (65-31-9)
22 Days in Alaska by Pamela Lanier (28-68-0)
22 Days in the American Southwest by R. Harris (28-88-5)
22 Days in Asia by R. Rapoport and B. Willes (65-17-3)
22 Days in Australia by John Gottberg (65-40-8)
22 Days in California by Roger Rapoport (28-93-1)
22 Days in China by Gaylon Duke and Zenia Victor (28-72-9)
22 Days in Dixie by Richard Polese (65-18-1)
22 Days in Europe by Rick Steves (65-05-X)
22 Days in Florida by Richard Harris (65-27-0)
22 Days in France by Rick Steves (65-07-6)
22 Days in Germany, Austria & Switzerland by R. Steves (65-39-4)
22 Days in Great Britain by Rick Steves (65-38-6)
22 Days in Hawaii by Arnold Schuchter (28-92-3)
22 Days in India by Anurag Mathur (28-87-7)

22 Days in Japan by David Old (28-73-7)
22 Days in Mexico by S. Rogers and T. Rosa (65-41-6)
22 Days in New England by Anne Wright (28-96-6)
22 Days in New Zealand by Arnold Schuchter (28-86-9)
22 Days in Norway, Denmark & Sweden by R. Steves (28-83-4)
22 Days in the Pacific Northwest by R. Harris (28-97-4)
22 Days in Spain & Portugal by Rick Steves (65-06-8)
22 Days in the West Indies by C. & S. Morreale (28-74-5)

All 22 Days titles are 128 to 152 pages and $7.95 each, except *22 Days Around the World*, which is 192 pages and $9.95.

"Kidding Around" Travel Guides for Children
Written for kids eight years of age and older. Generously illustrated in two colors with imaginative characters and images. An adventure to read and a treasure to keep.
Kidding Around Atlanta, Anne Pedersen (65-35-1) 64 pp. $9.95
Kidding Around London, Sarah Lovett (65-24-6) 64 pp. $9.95
Kidding Around Los Angeles, Judy Cash (65-34-3) 64 pp. $9.95
Kidding Around New York City, Sarah Lovett (65-33-5) 64 pp. $9.95
Kidding Around San Francisco, Rosemary Zibart (65-23-8) 64 pp. $9.95
Kidding Around Washington, D.C., Anne Pedersen (65-25-4) 64 pp. $9.95

Asia Through the Back Door, Rick Steves and John Gottberg (28-76-1) 336 pp. $13.95

Buddhist America: Centers, Retreats, Practices, Don Morreale (28-94-X) 400 pp. $12.95

Bus Touring: Charter Vacations, U.S.A., Stuart Warren (28-95-8) 168 pp. $9.95

Catholic America: Self-Renewal Centers and Retreats, Patricia Christian-Meyer (65-20-3) 325 pp. $13.95

Preconception: Preparing for Pregnancy and Parenthood, Brenda E. Aikey-Keller (65-44-0) 256 pp. $13.95

Complete Guide to Bed & Breakfasts, Inns & Guesthouses, Pamela Lanier (65-43-2) 520 pp. $14.95

Elderhostels: The Students' Choice, Mildred Hyman (65-28-9) 224 pp. $12.95

Europe 101: History & Art for the Traveler, Rick Steves and Gene Openshaw (28-78-8) 372 pp. $12.95

Europe Through the Back Door, Rick Steves (65-42-4) 404 pp. $14.95

Floating Vacations: River, Lake, and Ocean Adventures, Michael White (65-32-7) 256 pp. $17.95

Gypsying After 40: A Guide to Adventure and Self-Discovery, Bob Harris (28-71-0) 264 pp. $12.95

The Heart of Jerusalem, Arlynn Nellhaus (28-79-6) 312 pp. $12.95

Indian America: A Traveler's Companion, Eagle/Walking Turtle (65-29-7) 424 pp. $16.95

Mona Winks: Self-Guided Tours of Europe's Top Museums, Rick Steves (28-85-0) 450 pp. $14.95

The On and Off the Road Cookbook, Carl Franz (28-27-3) 272 pp. $8.50

The People's Guide to Mexico, Carl Franz (28-99-0) 608 pp. $15.95

The People's Guide to RV Camping in Mexico, Carl Franz with Steve Rogers (28-91-5) 256 pp. $13.95

Ranch Vacations: The Complete Guide to Guest and Resort, Fly-Fishing, and Cross-Country Skiing Ranches, Eugene Kilgore (65-30-0) 392 pp. $18.95

The Shopper's Guide to Mexico, Steve Rogers and Tina Rosa (28-90-7) 224 pp. $9.95

Ski Tech's Guide to Equipment, Skiwear, and Accessories, edited by Bill Tanler (65-45-9) 144 pp. $11.95

Ski Tech's Guide to Maintenance and Repair, edited by Bill Tanler (65-46-7) 144 pp. $11.95

Traveler's Guide to Asian Culture, Kevin Chambers (65-14-9) 224 pp. $13.95

Traveler's Guide to Healing Centers and Retreats in North America, Martine Rudee and Jonathan Blease (65-15-7) 240 pp. $11.95

Undiscovered Islands of the Caribbean, Burl Willes (28-80-X) 216 pp. $12.95

Automotive Repair Manuals

Each JMP automotive manual gives clear step-by-step instructions together with illustrations that show exactly how each system in the vehicle comes apart and goes back together. They tell everything a novice or experienced mechanic needs to know to perform periodic maintenance, tune-ups, trouble-shooting, and repair of the brake, fuel and emission control, electrical, cooling, clutch, transmission, driveline, steering, and suspension systems and even rebuild the engine.

How to Keep Your VW Alive (65-12-2) 424 pp. $19.95
How to Keep Your Rabbit Alive (28-47-8) 420 pp. $19.95
How to Keep Your Subaru Alive (65-11-4) 480 pp. $19.95
How to Keep Your Toyota Pickup Alive (28-81-3) 392 pp. $19.95
How to Keep Your Datsun/ Nissan Alive (28-65-6) 544 pp. $19.95

Other Automotive Books

The Greaseless Guide to Car Care Confidence: Take the Terror Out of Talking to Your Mechanic, Mary Jackson (65-19-X) 224 pp. $14.95
Off-Road Emergency Repair & Survival, James Ristow (65-26-2) 160 pp. $9.95
Road & Track's Used Car Classics, edited by Peter Bohr (28-69-9) 272 pp. $12.95

Ordering Information

If you cannot find our books in your local bookstore, you can order directly from us. Your books will be sent to you via UPS (for U.S. destinations), and you will receive them approximately 10 days from the time that we receive your order. Include $2.75 for the first item ordered and $.50 for each additional item to cover shipping and handling costs. UPS shipments to post office boxes take longer to arrive; if possible, please give us a street address. For airmail within the U.S., enclose $4.00 per book for shipping and handling. All foreign orders will be shipped surface rate. Please enclose $3.00 for the first item and $1.00 for each additional item. Please inquire for airmail rates.

Method of Payment

Your order may be paid by check, money order, or credit card. We cannot be responsible for cash sent through the mail. All payments must be made in U.S. dollars drawn on a U.S. bank. Canadian postal money orders in U.S. dollars are also acceptable. For VISA, MasterCard, or American Express orders, include your card number, expiration date, and your signature, or call (505)982-4078. Books ordered on American Express cards can be shipped only to the billing address of the cardholder. Sorry, no C.O.D.'s. Residents of sunny New Mexico, add 5.625% tax to the total.

Address all orders and inquiries to:
John Muir Publications
P.O. Box 613
Santa Fe, NM 87504
(505)982-4078